THE SERMON

THE SERMON

KEYS TO LIVING AN UNCOMMON LIFE FROM
THE SERMON ON THE MOUNT

DR. RON PHILLIPS
WITH DANA HARDING

Unless otherwise indicated, Scripture quotations are taken from the *New King James Version*. Copyright © 1979, 1980, 1982, 1990, 1995, Thomas Nelson, Inc. Publishers.

Scripture quotations marked *NIV* are taken from the Holy Bible, *New International Version*. *NIV* ® Copyright © 1973, 1978, 1984, 2011 by International Bible Society. Used by permission of Zondervan Publishing House. All right reserved.

Scripture quotations identified *MESSAGE* are from *THE MESSAGE*. Copyright © by Eugene H. Peterson 1993, 1994, 1995, 1996, 2000, 2001, 2001. Used by permission of NavPress. All rights reserved. Represented by Tyndale House Publishers, Inc.

Scripture quotations identified *KJV* are from the King James Version of the Bible.

Director of Publications: David W. Ray
Managing Editor of Publications: Lance Colkmire
Editorial Assistant: Elaine McDavid
Graphic Design and Layout: Michael McDonald

ISBN: 978-1-64288-083-0

Copyright © 2019 by Pathway Press
1080 Montgomery Avenue
Cleveland, Tennessee 37311

All rights reserved. No part of this publication may be reproduced or transmitted in any form or by any means, electronic or mechanical, including photocopying, recording, or otherwise, or by any information storage or retrieval system, without the permission in writing from the publisher. Please direct inquiries to Pathway Press, 1080 Montgomery Avenue, Cleveland, TN 37311.

Visit *www.pathwaypress.org* for more information.

Recommendations for
The Sermon

In *The Sermon*, Dr. Phillips presents insights from the Sermon on the Mount with anointing and clarity, showing us how Jesus' words still speak to us today as we seek to rise above the common and live extraordinary lives.

—Jentezen Franklin, Lead Pastor, Free Chapel

This book is truly an inspiring approach to revealing the heart of Jesus. Uniquely powerful and profound in so many wonderful ways.

—Ray Hughes

Dr. Ron Phillips reveals the true power of discipleship in Christ, as he expounds upon the truth and revelation that is found in the Sermon on the Mount. Taken from the greatest sermon ever to be preached, *The Sermon* will lead you step by step into the fullness of knowing Christ and having an intimate fellowship with the Holy Spirit. This is not for the faint-hearted! However, upon reading this book you will be challenged in every area of your life to live in the supernatural love of Christ, and a Kingdom mentality.

—Nathan Morris , Shake The Nations Ministries

I believe the Sermon on the Mount is the constitution and bylaws of the Kingdom. I have governed my life and ministry by the Beatitudes since the beginning of my ministry in 1970. My dear friend, Dr. Ron Phillips, in *The Sermon*, has taken me back again to the Mount to measure my progress. This book has the power and insight to change the White House, the courthouse, the schoolhouse and the church house but, most of all, your house.

—John Kilpatrick, Church of His Presence (Daphne, AL)

The Sermon can be looked at as a roadmap from a spiritual father to his sons and daughters to know how to navigate the narrow gate between religion and God's Kingdom. Kingdom living and a Kingdom mindset are polar opposites of religion; it is not legalism or logistics but is a mindset that is driven by God and the Holy Spirit that illuminates God's instruction and not only lights our paths but gives us spiritual strategies for success. Dr. Ron Phillips gleans from his personal walk with God and his years as a leader and shares his heartfelt stories and spiritual principles in a relational way that makes *The Sermon* attainable through this enjoyable read!

—*Rabbi Curt Landry, House of David (Fairland, OK)*

If this world's definition of the "good life" is fame, earthly notoriety, winning awards, then you had better pray to lose. There is a better life that exists without you or me at the center. The center piece of this new life is Christ Himself. This is the uncommon life—a life that is for everyone!

—*Eric Clark, Creative Church (Bluffton, SC)*

Dedications

From Ron Phillips

This work is dedicated to the all the unknown pastors who live faithfully and believe fervently in the Jesus lifestyle. To the thousands who have labored in a God's vineyard unheralded except in glory, blessed are you.

A special thank-you to my co-laborer, Dana Harding, for his contribution to this project. Without his tireless effort, this work would not have been completed. Well done, my friend!

From Dana Harding

To Julie: You have been my traveling partner for the last 26-plus years of this *Uncommon Life*. I wouldn't have it any other way. I love you.

To Bailey, Maddie, and Morgan: You all have taken the good with the bad, and travelled this uncommon road with Mom and I with grace and smiles. I'm so proud of the ladies you have become. Xo

To many friends and family members who have shaped the direction of my life: Your contribution to my walk with the Lord has meant everything to me. Your spirit and influence are represented here and in my heart, always.

Foreword

By anyone's account, it is the greatest sermon ever preached. On their very best days and with their very best efforts, two millennia of Gospel preachers have never been able to scratch the surface of the simple majesty of the Sermon on the Mount. It is an uncommon sermon preached by an uncommon Man presenting uncommon truths that result in an Uncommon Life. And this book that has sprung forth from our Savior's incomparable sermon is an uncommon book. *The Sermon* is the joint effort of two men: the godly pastor to and through whom the Lord gave these messages, and a member of his congregation whose life was changed radically by them.

Dr. Ron Phillips is a "preacher's preacher," a preacher *par excellence*. For more than thirty-eight years, the Word-hungry people of Abba's House in Hixson, Tennessee, never tired of hearing him proclaim the inexhaustible riches of Scripture. He is a master expositor who sows the truths he mines deep from God's Word deep into the hearts of his listeners with powerful presentation, effective illustrations, and relevant applications. For one year while I was in seminary in the 1980s and for seven years after my wife and I moved back to Chattanooga in 2010, I have been blessed to call him my pastor.

Dana Harding is a worshipper and an anointed worship leader. He is a master musician; in fact, his guitar skills are so advanced he could no doubt play in his choice of bands in the rock-music industry. Instead, he chooses to write, sing, and play music for his Savior. As you will learn in this book, he is a man who has passed through the furnace of affliction. Like Job of old, he emerged joyous after seeing the Lord as He really is (James 5:11). He now leads a truly Uncommon Life.

Before you turn the page, pause to open your heart and your mind to God's Spirit, and ask the Lord to change you as you feast on the milk and meat of the Word prepared so delightfully for you in this book. If you are mourning, you will be comforted; if you hunger and thirst for righteousness, you will be filled; if you are poor in spirit, you will receive the treasures of the kingdom of heaven as God's Spirit guides you through *The Sermon.*

—Dr. Randall Collins, Outline Bible Resources

Contents

Introduction 13

1. Growing Pains
—The Life that Never Stops Growing 17

2. Give Me a Break
—The Life that Is Merciful 31

3. Rise a Knight
—The Life Lived with Integrity 43

4. It's a Wonderful Life
—Living a Life of Lasting Influence 57

5. Back to the Future
—Embraces the Best of the Past 69

6. Heroes
—Life Lived from the Inside Out 81

7. Promises, Promises
—The Life that Keeps Its Promises 95

8. Great Expectations
—Goes Beyond what Is Expected 107

9. The Secret of Life
—Knows the Power of Sacred Secrets 119

10. The Nutritional Value of Soul Food
—The Life that Knows How to Pray 133

11. Life in the "Fast" Lane
—Willing to Do Without for Others 143

12. Treasure Island
—Winning the Battle Against Stuff 153

13. I Can See Clearly Now
—The Life that Has the Right Perspective 161

14. Who's the Boss?
—The Life that Knows Who Is in Charge 179

15. Mission Impossible?
—The Life that Refuses to Worry 189

16. In Search of . . .
— The Life that Lives with God's Priorities 199

17. Judgment Day
—The Life that Takes Off the Mask 211

18. Is Nothing Sacred?
—The Life That Respects the Sacred 221

19. Never Gonna Give You Up
—The Life that Never Quits 233

20. It's a Celebration
—The Life that Lives as a Son 243

21. The Secret of Success
—The Life that Is Well-Lived 253

22. You Have Chosen _____
—The Life that Journeys the Road Less Traveled 265

23. I Will Survive
—The Life that Seeks Lasting Results 275

24. Epilogue
—The Life that Is Uncommon 283

Introduction

What do you consider "uncommon"?

- An emergency worker who selflessly saves another person's life, perhaps giving up their own in the process?

- A baseball player who hits more homeruns that anyone in history?

- A rock singer who spends his time and money fighting disease in Third World countries?

- A figure in the shadows who rights wrongs, confronts evil, defeats the bad guys, and does it all while wearing a cape with his underwear on the outside?

Let's face it: While these people are to be commended for their actions (though perhaps not their attire), I believe that sometimes we make things much more difficult than they need to be. We make being "outstanding" or "uncommon" something that is to be achieved instead of lived on a daily basis. An Uncommon Life is for everyone, not just a select few athletes, artists, royals, or rocket scientists. Consider this quote by the late General Omar Bradley: "We have grasped the mystery of the atom and rejected the Sermon on the Mount."[1]

THE SERMON

The Sermon on the Mount

Perhaps the most profound teaching in history, these words of Jesus probably took Him less than 25 minutes to speak, and have resonated through the corridors of history for about 2000 years. However, this literary masterpiece, which has been referred to as the "Manifesto of the Kingdom," and the "Magna Carta of the Kingdom" (for all your history buffs), is more than just a "good read"—it is a way of life.

It is the "free prize inside." It is treasure at the end of the rainbow in our search for significance. It is the gateway to the Uncommon Life.

"So," you may inquire, "what does the Sermon on the Mount have to do with living an Uncommon Life?"

I'm glad you asked!

There is within each of us a desire to be significant and even extraordinary. If we are all honest with ourselves, we would probably admit to asking the question, "Can my life be different and make a difference?"

The answer: *Absolutely!* True happiness, real significance, and profound purpose can be experienced and enjoyed by anyone willing to embrace the liberty and freedom outlined in this text. In its words is contained a clear portrayal of the Uncommon Life.

However, like anything you might consider uncommon or extraordinary, there is a catch.

The Uncommon Life clashes with 21st-century culture. It collides with our shallow lifestyles. It challenges our ideas of "ideal." It puts to shame what has become a culturally corrupt version of Christianity.

Putting General Bradley's quote a different way: *We have struggled, searched, and studied to unlock the mystery of making the*

Interoduction

atomic bomb. Yet, the very simple teaching that would help us avoid war in the first place, a teaching available to everyone, has collected dust on the shelves of nearly every home in America.

- Our shallow efforts at happiness are exposed by the Sermon on the Mount.

- Our definitions of *integrity* and *positive character* are shattered by the Sermon on the Mount.

- Our lack of patience is uncovered by the Sermon on the Mount.

- Our moral decline and materialism are confronted by the Sermon on the Mount.

- The weak foundations of a culture built on pretense and self-interest are obliterated by the Sermon on the Mount.

Not bad for a 25-minute speech!

But wait! There's more! With this sermon, you'll also receive a better life! A life that rises from the ashes of being crushed and smashed to being healed and helped. A life filled with joy, blessing, and significance. A life that is uncommon.

The Uncommon Life does not rise from within the culture. The Uncommon Life changes and transforms the culture.

I believe that what we find in the Sermon on the Mount are keys that unlock the gateway to the Uncommon Life—*twenty-three keys*, to be exact. These are twenty-three simple actions that release a life of promise and fulfillment right here, right now.

The Uncommon Life . . .

- never stops growing
- gives others some slack

THE SERMON

- lives with intensity and integrity
- has lasting influence
- embraces the best of the past
- operates from the inside out
- keeps its promises
- goes beyond what is expected
- knows the power of sacred secrets
- knows how to pray
- will do without for others
- wins the battle against more stuff
- looks for the best
- knows who is the Boss
- does not worry
- has the right priorities
- takes off the mask
- respects what is sacred
- refuses to give up
- lives like a son, not a slave
- practices the Golden Rule
- journeys on the road less traveled
- will survive and thrive.

These concepts are yours for the taking—keys to a better life. Twenty-three golden keys to unlock an Uncommon Life.

Chapter 1
GROWING PAINS
The Life that Never Stops Growing

And seeing the multitudes, He went up on a mountain, and when He was seated His disciples came to Him. Then He opened His mouth and taught them saying:

"Blessed are the poor in spirit, for theirs is the kingdom of Heaven.

Blessed are those who mourn, for they shall be comforted.

Blessed are the meek, for they shall inherit the earth.

Blessed are those who hunger and thirst for righteousness, for they shall be filled."

—Matthew 5:1-6

The Sermon on the Mount starts off, not with hidden treasure, but with a valuable jewel in plain view; the "Hope Diamond" of the Sermon on the Mount.

The Beatitudes

The *Merriam-Webster Dictionary* defines *beatitude* as "a state of utmost bliss." You might say that beatitudes are attitudes of being—attitudes that should exude from the life of anyone who is a sold-out believer in Jesus Christ. These eight attitudes of being are like the

THE SERMON

facets of a beautiful diamond. When all eight of these attitudes are working together, allowing the light (or virtues) of Christ to shine through, the result is a prism of color, light, and beauty that is evident to anyone who comes near. These virtues were what the Apostle Paul was referring to when he talked about *"the measure of the stature of the fullness of Christ"* (Ephesians 4:13).

- Jesus was poor in spirit.

- Jesus mourned over broken people.

- Jesus was meek, and never tried to "make a name for Himself."

- Jesus suffered for righteousness' sake (as well as ours).

But what we see here in these first four beatitudes is a contradiction in terms, the first of many that will fly in the face of the contemporary mindset. This is the picture of the "happy life." True happiness cannot be bought with money, fame, prestige, or power. Yes, I will grant you that those things give a temporary high, but what happens when . . .

- the money is gone?

- the fresher, younger, prettier face shows up on the scene?

- the limelight shifts with the latest definition of *cool, chic,* or *hot?*

- the ambition and ecstasy of being at the top aren't enough to keep you there anymore?

Where is the guarantee? Where is the warranty? Who do we return it to when the parts begin to fall off the cheap imitation of a fulfilling life that we allowed the "self-absorbed philosophy of the world" to shape us into?

To shape us into—do you see that? That's the secret. True happiness begins on the inside, and works its way out. It isn't shaped by any external forces. It does the shaping. It forms us into something that is impervious to a world bent on pressuring us into a mold of conformity and compromise.

And it starts with pain.

Now wait. Before you reach for the aspirin or the icepack, let me explain. First, we have to get out of the mindset that all pain is bad. Pain can be a very useful tool, when appreciated and respected for what it does.

- Pain lets us know we are growing (growing-pains).

- Pain lets us know we are hungry (hunger pangs)

- Pain tells us when our body needs a rest or a break (hopefully, before we break).

- Pain warns us of an imminent threat.

Throughout the stories in the Bible, we hear a lot about a disease known as leprosy. One of the interesting things about leprosy, and what makes it such a terrible affliction, is that it takes away the sensation of pain from the person who has been affected. Because of the lack of feeling, the person cannot sense when they are burned or cut (or worse). The body's mechanism for warning against danger is broken, and the leper cannot feel when disease and deterioration eat away at him.

So, we can agree that pain is, in many cases, a useful indicator that we are, in fact, healthy. It lets us know that we are growing. Just by taking a look at nature, we can learn a very valuable principle:

If we are not growing, we are dying.

Think about it. What tree, bush, or blade of grass ever stays exactly the way it is year after year? If a tree or bush doesn't bloom, it doesn't get nourishment from the surrounding environment. If a plant doesn't receive the nutrients it needs through blooming and growing, it withers up and dies. The same is true for us, and we see it plainly in the first four beatitudes. We see a person who is hungry and growing, a person who knows that they have not "arrived." We see a person who, regardless of age, knows there is more ahead on the road of life. This hungry soul is not satisfied with the accomplishments of yesterday. It is always looking for the ways to keep moving forward. We have to open ourselves up to the challenges that life brings in order to grow in the grace and faith that God calls us to.

These first four attitudes work together to reveal the *first key to an Uncommon Life.* These first four principles lay the foundation upon which the rest of the Sermon on the Mount is built. So, let's start building! The growing person knows how you enter the Kingdom.

YOU ENTER THE KINGDOM EMPTY-HANDED.

"Happy are the helpless."

As the old saying goes, "You can't take it with you."

It is the opposite of self-sufficiency, and the mindset of "Get all you can, can all you get, and sit on the lid." It is the attitude that, in God's eternal balance, we are all poverty-stricken.

The "poor in spirit" or "helpless" see themselves as objects of God's grace without which they would have nothing, would be nothing, and could hope for nothing. Here is a person who has come to understand that God is all, and is in all. He knows that he is totally dependent upon God for everything, in every area of his life.

Rich Mullins was one of the most successful songwriters in Christian music in the late 20th century. His songs have been recorded by such artists as Amy Grant, Jars of Clay, Michael W. Smith, and John Tesh. His song "Awesome God" is one of the most well-known contemporary Christian songs of all time. Rich had it made. He had "arrived" in an industry that can be a tough nut to crack. Yet, at the time of his death in 1997, Rich lived in a hogan on a Navajo reservation where he taught music to Navajo children. The money he made from royalties for his writing went to his church, where they paid Rich an "average annual salary," and gave the rest away. [2]

What makes someone like Rich do something so seemingly "radical"?

Rich once said, *"Jesus said whatever you do to the least of these My brothers, you've done it to Me. And this is what I've come to think. That if I want to identify fully with Jesus Christ, who I claim to be my Savior and Lord, the best way that I can do that is to identify with the poor."* [3]

Rich got it. We are all poor.

I don't care who you are. I don't care how much money you make. I don't care how many times your face graces the covers of magazines in grocery-store checkout lines. You are poor.

Let's face it:

- You can't buy love.

- You can't make the rain fall.

- You can't stop the relentless march of time.

- You can't be sure of another breath, much less another day.

However, happiness comes in this realization. Happiness comes to the person who understands that, without the presence of God in his life,

THE SERMON

real happiness is not possible. He sees this as his continuing position, and finds blessing with this as his daily and constant attitude. This attitude stands in stark contrast to the one that no longer sees the need for God, and depends solely on the individual to "make it happen" in his life.

The Bible tells us of two men who went up to pray. One man said, "God, I thank You I am not like other men." The other man prayed, "God, be merciful to me, a sinner." The second man realized that he lacked something that he had no power to provide for himself, something that only God could supply (see Luke 18:10-14).

Do you have any idea that, no matter how much you may have, your debt of sin makes you a beggar at the throne of grace? This principle is summed up very well in the lyrics of a beloved hymn, "Rock of Ages":

Nothing in my hand I bring,

Simply to Thy cross I cling.

Helpless look to Thee for grace,

Naked come to Thee for dress. [4]

The helpless have genuine happiness, bliss, and joy. The helpless possess the Kingdom of Heaven, and are already subjects of this Kingdom. They enjoy it, live in it, enjoy the privileges of it, and look forward to the culmination of it.

YOU ENTER THE KINGDOM WITH A TENDER HEART.

"Blessed are the heartbroken."

"Blessed are they that mourn."

This is the opposite of self-centeredness. The person of this world has no time to weep over sin, nor the heartbreak of others.

This approach to life is dry-eyed, cold-hearted, and square-jawed. It has no compassion to offer. Christian people hear the call of a world screaming, "Enjoy!" Christ says, "Grieve!" You could put it another way: *Happy is the man who is bankrupt and the man who is brokenhearted.*

The mourner makes it a practice to share his neighbor's sorrow. The story is told in Swiss history that, during the Battle of Sempach (1386), the army of the Old Swiss Confederacy was on the verge of defeat. The short swords and spears of the Swiss army were no match for the long spears and pikes of their Austrian foes. Somehow, they needed to break through the impenetrable line if they were to have any hope of defeating their invaders. A man by the name of Arnold von Winkelreid stepped from among the ranks of the Swiss. Knowing what needed to be done, and at what cost, he charged the enemy lines with arms outstretched, pulling the enemy spears into his own body as he ran, and opening up a hole in the Austrian line through which the Swiss were able to charge, beating back the Austrians, and winning a decisive victory for the Swiss.

How we need to feel the spears of sorrow and pain that our neighbors bear. We are to mourn over sin. It seems that there are fewer and fewer people who care what sin is doing to our world. Where are the people with the heart of Jeremiah, who wept over the sins of Israel? Where are the people with the heart of Jesus, who wept over the sins of Jerusalem? Look at our old world, with its imperfections, injustices, wrongs, and problems. It is filled with suffering and death, with the righteous suffering and dying alongside of the unrighteous. And the reason for this can be summed up in one word: *sin.* Not until we learn to weep over the ruins of a society torn apart by ungodliness will we *ever* experience the comfort of God.

Mourning is evidence of spiritual life, a sign that the mourner can still feel pain. Father Damien (January 3, 1840—April 15, 1889) was a Belgian priest who, upon visiting a Christian shrine, asked to be able to serve as a missionary for twelve years. During his twelfth year of serving at a leper colony in Molokai, Hawaii, he contracted the most-deadly form of the disease, succumbing to it four years later. He had said that he knew he had caught the dreaded disease when he spilled boiling water on himself, and could not feel it. [5]

How sad it is when we allow our hearts to grow cold and insensitive, and no longer feel pain—our own or the pain of those around us.

However, we can find a reason to be thankful for a broken heart. It is through that breaking that we discover the path to Calvary. Revelation 7:17 tells us God is the great Comforter who wipes away all tears from our eyes. The word *comfort* is the Greek word *paraclete*. It means "one who intercedes," or "the one called alongside to give us strength." But it is more than a title or position, it is a promise of comfort from God.

YOU ENTER THE KINGDOM ON BENDED KNEES.

"Happy are the humble."

Meekness is not weakness.

Reggie was a walking contradiction. He was what you might call "the local boy who made good." A good-natured man with an infectious smile, he was, at the least, an imposing figure. The "average" person who stood next to him was dwarfed by his size. When he took your hand to greet you, you almost wondered if you'd ever get it back; your hand would seemingly disappear into his. As a minister of the Gospel, he was not afraid to share the love of Jesus with people around him, and did so, whether at church, with friends, or at work.

Work? Yes, Reggie had another job. He was also a minister of another sort. On the job, his reputation as "The Minister of Defense" was a well-earned moniker, which anyone who ever faced him on the gridiron would readily admit. Reggie, on a football field, was poetry in motion. But the performers in this ballet were not 90-pound ballerinas; they were 250-pound NFL offensive linemen with one thought on their minds: *Protect the guy with the football.* Yet, if you had the misfortune of having to line up facing Reggie, the chances were good that you were about to learn the difference between meekness and weakness. As a Super Bowl champion who, upon his retirement, held the NFL all-time sack record, Reggie White proved there is a big difference between spiritual meekness and physical weakness. [6]

The most common definition of *meekness* is simple: "being humble-minded." Moses was called a meek man, as well as Jesus. Meekness is the opposite of the prideful self-assertiveness we see wielded by powerful conquerors throughout history. Men like Genghis Khan, Napoleon, Julius Caesar, and Alexander the Great possessed pride and strength enough to conquer the world, but not to hold it. "Quiet humility" defines the person who has surrendered his life to Jesus Christ. This meek individual knows that God gives him power, as well as molds his life. This is spelled out in Psalm 37. He has committed his way to Christ, and God is directing his path.

The earth will belong to the meek and humble servant of Christ, not the brazen conqueror.

YOU ENTER THE KINGDOM WITH A HUNGRY SOUL.

"Happy are the hungering."

As we grow in Christ, the appetites of the Kingdom citizen change.

THE SERMON

A desire for the unsatisfying "fast food" of the world is changed into a hunger for the rich, slow-cooked, deep-fried banquet laid out before us at the table of our Heavenly Father—a more lasting, savory menu than the world could ever produce.

Righteousness is the gift of Jesus Christ to all of those who come to Him for forgiveness. It is not something we deserve, earn, or work toward, but rather the free gift of God that transfers the character of His Son, Jesus, into our spiritual DNA. When God looks at us, He sees Jesus!

It was a guarantee given to Job: *"He shall pray to God, and He will delight in him, he shall see His face with joy, for He restores to man His righteousness"* (Job 33:26).

It was a hope that David believed: *"Hear me when I call, O God of my righteousness! You have relieved me in my distress; have mercy upon me, and hear my prayer"* (Psalm 4:1).

It was a gift that Paul understood: *"For if by the one man's offense death reigned through the one, much more those who receive abundance of grace and of the gift of righteousness will reign in life through the One, Jesus Christ"* (Romans 5:17).

Here is a hunger that leaves one unsatisfied with a life that is less than it could be. Here is a life made sick by trying to satisfy life's hunger with the "junk food" of sin, habits, and wrong choices that do nothing but destroy a healthy spirit. Here is a person who, after throwing up from indulging in the à-la-carte menu of worldly desires, is now consumed with a gnawing hunger deep inside that nothing in this world can satisfy. At the end of the day, when you push away from the table, you may discover, as the prodigal son did, that the world's fare was a feast fit for a pig, and nothing more.

But when he came to himself, he said, *"How many of my father's hired servants have bread enough and to spare, and I perish with hunger?"* (Luke 15:17).

The growing pains in his belly were the greatest hunger that ever happened to this boy. It was that hunger that drove him home where he discovered, after sampling all the world could offer, that what truly satisfied was the bread he found at his father's table.

And Jesus said to them, *"I am the bread of life. He who comes to Me shall never hunger, and he who believes in Me shall never die"* (John 6:35).

When we come to Jesus, our days of spiritual hunger and thirst are over. After all, God had a purpose and a plan in allowing that hunger in the first place.

"So He humbled you, allowed you to hunger, and fed you with manna which you did not know nor did your fathers know, that He might make you know that man shall not live by bread alone; but man lives by every word that proceeds from the mouth of the Lord" (Deuteronomy 8:3).

God wants you to learn that you need Him!

She had been married multiple times. She was shacked-up with a man she wasn't married to. She had probably been both perpetrator and victim in a series of relationships that are the stuff soap operas are made of. Yet, she lived two thousand years ago, and although we don't know her name, we do know what Jesus said to her; words that are as valid now as they were when He spoke them, sitting by the edge of a well in Israel on a hot afternoon.

THE SERMON

Jesus answered and said to her, *"Whoever drinks of this water will thirst again, but whoever drinks of the water that I shall give him will never thirst. But the water that I shall give him will become in him a fountain of water springing up into everlasting life"* (John 4:13-14).

Scripture is filled with the sounds of hungry, thirsty people. Throughout its pages resound the cries of people parched from spiritual drought, knowing there is only one thing that can satisfy.

It's in the song of the musician-poet who said, *"As the deer pants for the water brooks, so pants my soul for You, O God"* (Psalm 42:1).

It's in the quiet meditation of a mighty king who said, *"O God, You are my God; Early will I seek You; My soul thirsts for You; My flesh longs for You in a dry and thirsty land, where there is no water"* (Psalm 63:1).

It's in the cry of a prophet declaring, *"Ho! Everyone who thirsts, come to the waters; and you who have no money, come, buy and eat. Yes, come, buy wine and milk without money and without price"* (Isaiah 55:1).

It's in the resonant frequencies of the Voice as the sound of many waters, saying, *"It is done! I am the Alpha and the Omega, the Beginning and the End. I will give of the fountain of the water of life freely to him who thirsts"* (Revelation 21:6).

So, what can we conclude?

Life is more than money. It's not about Grammy Awards, Super Bowl rings, being number one, and living the "good" life. It's *all* about living the "better" life—a life that has Jesus Christ at the center. It's about being genuinely happy; happiness brought about by a hunger to be right with God, and to see those around you right with God.

It's about a dependence on God, evidenced by compassion for others, humility, and an overwhelming desire for God's righteousness to prevail. This is the portrait of the person who has discovered abiding happiness and abounding joy.

Does this picture resemble you?

THE SERMON

KEY QUESTIONS TO PONDER
Chapter 1: *Growing Pains*

1. Read the Beatitudes (Matthew 5:1-12).

- Discuss why they are called the "secret to true happiness."

- How do the first four beatitudes contradicts contemporary thinking?

2. Discuss the following statement: "Pain can be a useful tool, when appreciated and respected for what it does."

- How does pain factor into our growth?

- Why can't we grow as a Christian without pain? (See John 15.)

3. What did Jesus mean when He said, *"Blessed are the meek, for they shall inherit the earth"* (Matthew 5:5)?

- What does a "meek" person look like? Name someone in your life you consider "meek."

- Name the Biblical character (besides Jesus) who was considered the "meekest" man on the earth (see Numbers 12:3). How was this man meek?

Chapter 2
GIVE ME A BREAK
The Life that Is Merciful

"Blessed are the merciful, for they will be shown mercy."

—Matthew 5:7 (NIV)

In the song "To Forgive" by Steve Taylor, he asks, *"Oh, will we live to forgive?"*

A good song with a strong message about forgiveness. We'll get back to that in a minute.

We have already established that God is a "happy God." The things that Jesus taught His disciples directed them to that joy. In John 15:11, Jesus told them, *"These things I have spoken to you, that My joy may remain in you, and that your joy may be full."* In the first four Beatitudes, happiness belongs to those who know that their inadequacies are met by Christ, that their comfort comes from the Holy Spirit, and that only Jesus can satisfy their deep hunger and quench their deep thirst.

However, now let's pause and take a look at one single Beatitude: *"Blessed are the merciful, for they shall obtain mercy."* But, let's say it another way so our 21st-century minds can really grasp: *"Happy are the merciful, for they will come into possession of mercy."*

THE SERMON

Perhaps the greatest foe of real happiness and the blessings that God has in store for His children is a hardened heart that cannot show mercy and forgive.

THE DEFINITION OF MERCY

The word *mercy* means "pity, compassion, sympathy." It is the ability to get into another person's skin, and feel what they feel. Instead of judging, condemning, and not forgiving, the person who exhibits mercy looks with a tender and compassionate heart upon others. William Penn, a founding father of the State of Pennsylvania, once said, "Kings in this world should imitate God, their mercy should be above their works." [8]

William Penn understood the importance of rulers and those in authority to exhibit mercy to those they rule, and even sit in judgment over.

On October 2, 2006, Charles Carl Roberts IV walked into the West Nickel Mines School in Bart Township of Lancaster County, Pennsylvania. After asking a seemingly trivial question to some of those inside the small, Amish school, he walked out to his truck, then returned, brandishing a 9mm handgun. Once inside, he released some male students and parents, but kept a number of female hostages before barricading himself and his victims inside the small building. Within an hour, shots were fired, and when the police stormed the building, they found ten girls shot execution-style, and Roberts himself lying dead from a single, self-inflicted gunshot wound. Of the ten girls shot, five died from their injuries. Some of the survivors suffer from permanent physical disabilities to this day. The age ranges of the victims were six to thirteen years of age. [9]

The aftermath of this massacre, however, was almost as shocking to those in the media as the event itself. The response to the events of October 2 was an outpouring of unbridled mercy and forgiveness, not just to the perpetrator of this heinous act, but to his family as well. Within hours of the horrific event, people from the Amish community visited the Roberts family, offering them comfort, forgiveness, and hope. It was said that one Amish man held Roberts' devastated father in his arms for an hour as the man cried over what his son had done. At Roberts' funeral, the Amish people in attendance outnumbered the non-Amish. Marie Roberts, the killer's widow, was one of the only "outsiders" invited to the funeral of one of the victims. The Amish community even went as far as to set up a charitable fund for the Roberts family.[10] The Amish people in that community met a diabolical act of aggression and violence with an unfathomable presentation of mercy and forgiveness that could not be denied, ignored, or forgotten.

THE SOURCE OF MERCY

God, our Father, exudes mercy. His throne in Israel on top of the Ark of the Covenant was called the *mercy seat*. In Leviticus 16:2, God promised Moses that He would *"appear in the cloud above the mercy seat."* Once a year, the High Priest would enter the Holy of Holies in the Tabernacle, and would apply the blood of the sacrifice to the mercy seat for forgiveness of sins for the people of God. How incredible it is for us now, because of the blood of Jesus, to be able to enter into His presence, not once a year, but 24 hours a day, 7 days a week, 365 days a year!

There is no end to God's mercy. Psalm 100:5 says, *"The Lord is good; His mercy is everlasting, and His truth endures to all generations."*

THE SERMON

God is the Father of mercy, as described in 2 Corinthians 1:3: *"Blessed be the God and Father of our Lord Jesus Christ, the Father of mercies and God of all comfort."*

God is rich in mercy. His mercy cannot be exhausted. Ephesians 2:4-5 says, *"God, who is rich in mercy, because of His great love with which He loved us, even when we were dead in trespasses, made us alive together with Christ."*

The apostle James put it this way: *"But the wisdom that is from above is first pure, then peaceable, gentle, willing to yield, full of mercy and good fruits, without partiality and without hypocrisy"* (James 3:17).

God is the definitive authority on mercy. He sits on a throne called "Mercy"; is the Father of mercy; is rich in mercy; and pours out mercy.

THE EXPERIENCE OF MERCY

There can be no question that each of us has received mercy. Were this not the case, we would all be on our way to Hell. But God, as the Father of mercy, has heaped mercy upon us. God got into our skin through His Son, Jesus of Nazareth. He became one of us, experienced our temptations, cried at our sorrow, and felt our pain. Finally, in great mercy, Jesus died to save us.

> *Not by works of righteousness which we have done, but according to His mercy He saved us, through the washing of regeneration and renewing of the Holy Spirit* (Titus 3:5).

In the story of the prodigal son (Luke 15:11-31), Jesus tells us that, once the younger son had gone through his inheritance, lost everything, had been deserted by his fair-weather friends, and was sharing a less-than-kosher dinner with less-than-kosher dinner guests, this wayward young man came to himself. He remembered that his father's own servants were treated better than he was being treated now. He knew that they were eating food fit for a king. He recognized the difference between eating *from* the menu and eating *with* the menu. He realized all of this because of one thing—the experience of mercy.

I'm sure he recollected times when, as a small boy, he saw his older brother or a family servant disobey his father. And no doubt he, too, had disobeyed. He probably remembered how his father corrected or chastised the guilty party, only to follow that up with unconditional love and mercy. His past experience with the mercy of his father led him to a conclusion: *If I go to my father, and throw myself at his mercy, even though I know he won't take me back as a son, maybe I can get job as a hired hand.* He then left the pigpen, and started the long journey home.

It is important to note that mercy did not seek him out. Verse 20 says the father *saw him while he was still a long way off,* not *the father went and sought him out.* Mercy has a drawing effect on the one in need of it. There is an attraction to mercy that is instilled through experience. The father knew the son remembered the way home, and at some point, would set his foot solidly on the path of return. And it was the memory of that mercy that was the still, small voice calling to the son once he hit rock-bottom.

Once we truly experience the mercy of God, we will always have that beacon to guide us to His heart. As the hymn says:

> *Mercy there was great, and grace was free;*
> *Pardon there was multiplied to me;*

THE SERMON

There my burdened soul found liberty
At Calvary.[11]

THE EXPRESSION OF MERCY

What God bestows on us will show on us! Once we have received mercy, it is our obligation to show mercy. Mercy is a gift of the Spirit. In Romans 12, Paul outlines the gifts of the Spirit, and the responsibility that comes with each gift. In verse 8, he says: *"If it is encouraging, then give encouragement; if it is giving, then give generously; if it is to lead, do it diligently; if it is to show mercy, do it cheerfully"* (NIV).

Mercy must always be associated with humility. Just a few verses before, Paul says: *"Do not think of yourself more highly than you ought, but rather think of yourself with sober judgment, in accordance with the faith God has distributed to each of you"* (v. 3 NIV).

Paul recognized the more faith we are given, our awareness of the precious gift of mercy increases. This prompts genuine humility, not just toward our own circumstances, but also in the manner in which we treat others. John Bradford, an English reformer, was imprisoned in the Tower of London. One day, he observed another prisoner being lead to his execution. Bradford is said to have exclaimed, "There, but for the grace of God, goes John Bradford!" All of us are required to express mercy toward others. Displaying mercy means we have experienced mercy. However, even the most seemingly religious can lack this attitude.

"Woe to you, scribes and Pharisees, hypocrites! For you pay of tithe mint and anise and cummin, and have neglected the weightier matters of the law: justice and mercy and faith. These you ought to

have done, without leaving the others undone" (Matthew 23:23). In this verse, Jesus was scathing in His rebuke of the Pharisees for lacking mercy. When we turn to Matthew 18, we are shaken by what comes from the lips of Jesus:

> *Then Peter came to Him and said, "Lord, how often shall my brother sin against me, and I forgive him? Up to seven times?" Jesus said to him, "I do not say to you, up to seven times, but up to seventy times seven"* (vv. 21-22).

Jesus is declaring we cannot put a limit on forgiveness. He then told about a man who owed a fortune he could not repay, and was on the verge of being sold, along with his family, into slavery. Although we are not sure of exactly what the amount would have been in today's terms, it is suggested that "ten thousand talents" was easily in the millions, if not billions, of dollars. The man went before the king, to whom he owed the money, and begged for mercy. The king had compassion on the man, and forgave him.

> *"The servant therefore fell down before him, saying, 'Master, have patience with me, and I will pay you all.' Then the master of that servant was moved with compassion, released him, and forgave him the debt"* (vv. 26-27).

So, at this point, we can assume the forgiven man left the king's presence, jumping for joy, ran down the street, gathered his friends around him, and told all of them what the merciful king had done, right?

Wrong. The Bible tells us the man went out and "found" a man who owed him some money. By saying "found," that would seem to

THE SERMON

indicate the man went out looking for him. Jesus says the amount in question was a hundred denarii which, some scholars estimate, was the equivalent of about seventeen dollars. When the man could not pay back the debt, the servant (formerly known as "Forgiven"), had him thrown into prison.

Well, good news travels fast . . . and bad news travels faster.

There were others around who saw what happened, and knew the debt the servant (formerly known as Forgiven; currently known as "Foolish") had been absolved of. They went straight back to the king, and told him the whole story.

Jesus continues the parable: *"Then his master, after he had called him, said to him, 'You wicked servant! I forgave you all that debt because you begged me. Should you not also have compassion on your fellow servant, just as I had pity on you?' And his master was angry, and delivered him to the torturers until he should pay all that was due him"* (vv. 32-34).

But then Jesus fired the proverbial "shot across the bow" at His disciples with verse 35: *"So My heavenly Father also will do to you if each of you, from his heart, does not forgive his brother his trespasses."*

Not being able to show mercy may be a telling testimony that one has not truly forgiven. Take a look a James 2:13: *"For judgment is without mercy to the one who has shown no mercy. Mercy triumphs over judgment."*

God will judge without mercy those who show no mercy. Yet, for those who show mercy, they are free from judgment. Forgiveness is the litmus test for mercy. The Lord's Prayer includes the command to forgive: *"And forgive us our debts, as we forgive our debtors. And do not lead us into temptation, but deliver us from the evil one. For Yours is the kingdom, and the power, and the glory forever. Amen"* (Matthew 6:12-13).

At this point, most of us are saying "If we could just stop there." But, no, Jesus goes on in verses 14 and 15: *"For if you forgive men their trespasses, your heavenly Father will also forgive you. But if you do not forgive men their trespasses, neither will your heavenly Father forgive your trespasses."*

What starts as the "model prayer" ends with a horrifying ultimatum: *Forgive, or you will not be forgiven.*

On May 13, 1981, as the motorcade of Pope John Paul II was passing through the streets of Vatican City, a Turkish assassin by the name of Mehmet Ali Ağca opened fire on the pontiff, striking him four times. The shooter was immediately apprehended, and over the course of the next several hours, Pope John Paul lost nearly three quarters of his blood, and went through five hours of emergency surgery.[12]

However, following the attempt on his life, the Pope issued a statement concerning his would-be assassin: "Pray for my brother, whom I have sincerely forgiven."

In 1983, Pope John Paul II visited Ağca at the prison in Rome where he was being held, and the two seemingly developed a friendship. The Pope had meetings with both Ağca's mother and brother, and eventually petitioned the president of Italy for the release of Ağca from prison in Rome, which was granted in 2000.[13]

THE SERMON

Steve Taylor's song "To Forgive" includes a reference to "an indelible mark" remaining following a shooting.

Which was the more indelible mark that was left following the shooting of the Pope? Was it the scars left by the bullets from Ağca's gun, or the mark of absolution and freedom left by someone who understood the power contained in the ability to forgive?

Your soul's condition can be diagnosed by how you forgive.

KEY QUESTIONS TO PONDER
Chapter 2: *Give Me a Break*

1. Discuss Romans 12:8 in light of the following statement: "What God bestows on us will show on us! Once we have received mercy, it is our obligation to show mercy."

2. How many times did Jesus say to Peter we must forgive? (See Matthew 18:21.) Is that a literal number? If not, is there an actual number?

3. Read the parable in Matthew 18:23-35. In light of Jesus' teaching, why should I show mercy to someone who has hurt me?

Chapter 3
RISE A KNIGHT
The Life Lived with Integrity

"Blessed are the merciful, for they will be shown mercy.

Blessed are the pure in heart, for they will see God.

Blessed are the peacemakers, for they will be called children of God.

Blessed are those who are persecuted for righteousness, for theirs is the kingdom of heaven.

Blessed are you when people insult you, persecute you and falsely say all kinds of evil against you because of Me. Rejoice and be glad, because great is your reward in heaven, for in the same way they persecuted the prophets who were before you."

—Matthew 5:7-12 (NIV)

The movie *Kingdom of Heaven* is a loose retelling of the fall of Jerusalem in 1187. Balian, the hero of the movie, is inheriting the title "Baron of Ibelin" from his dying father, Godfrey. Rising from his deathbed to pass on his title, Godfrey charges his kneeling son:

> *"Be without fear in the face of your enemies. Be brave and upright, that God may love thee. Speak the truth always, even if it leads to your death. Safeguard the helpless*

THE SERMON

*and do no wrong; that is your oath." Without warning,
Godfrey then reaches out and slaps Balian in the face.*

*"And that is so you remember it. Rise a knight . . .
rise a knight!"* [14]

With that, Godfrey calls Balian to a life of integrity.

It has been said that *integrity* is "who you are when no one is watching." Former U.S. Senator Alan K. Simpson once said, "If you have integrity, nothing else matters. If you don't have integrity, nothing else matters."[15]

The first four Beatitudes set forth the inner character of the Kingdom citizen. The last four are the outward expression of the Kingdom life. The one who has known poverty of spirit, bowed bankrupt before a Holy God, repented in godly sorrow for sin, and hungered for God will be known of Him. The Kingdom citizen will not only be known of God, but will express the life of God to others. Each one of these four "attitudes of being" is an expression of the life of Christ poured out through the individual.

The first four Beatitudes are the initial exercises of the heart toward God—the natural responses of a heart that has truly come into contact with His holy nature. The last four are the fruit of that encounter. The new believer, having hungered and thirsted for God, is now filled to overflowing with the life of God. The last four Beatitudes give us the distinguishing marks of the Kingdom citizen.

SAFEGUARD THE HELPLESS (Unconventional Mercy)

"Blessed are the merciful." Mercy is the bloom that grows on the stem of a righteous life. The word *mercy* means "pity, sympathy, compassion." It is the ability to get inside another person's skin, and

feel what he feels. If *grace* is "receiving what we don't deserve," then *mercy* is "not receiving what we do deserve."

Christ in us is the source of mercy. Mercy is an integral part of the nature of God. In 2 Corinthians 1:3, Paul calls Him the *"Father of mercy,"* and refers to Him as *"rich in mercy"* in Ephesians 2:4. James 3:17 describes the wisdom that emanates from the heart of God as being *"full of mercy."*

If we are to have any hope of living with integrity, we must come to the realization that, as recipients of mercy, we have to be willing to give mercy. In the words of James, "Mercy triumphs over judgment!" When Jesus takes up residence in our lives, He brings mercy with Him, and desires to make that mercy pour out of our lives.

Our Lord says our ability to show mercy indicates whether or not we have received mercy. The rich man in Hell (Luke 16) begged for mercy, but in life, he had not been merciful to the poor. Mercy is the gift of God.

Queen Victoria reigned as the British monarch for over 60 years. During that time, she had developed a friendship with Principal John Tulloch, and his wife, of St. Mary's College. In 1861, the queen's husband, Prince Albert, passed away in his prime (he was only 42). Having loved her husband very much, the queen mourned his death for years. Several years later, Principal Tulloch passed away, leaving Mrs. Tulloch all alone. One day, without warning, Queen Victoria visited Mrs. Tulloch at her home. As the grieving widow struggled to rise to show proper respect, Queen Victoria approached her and said, "My dear, don't rise. I am not coming to you today as the queen to her subject, but as one woman who has lost her husband to another."

There is an old saying, "It takes one to know one." The life that has truly received mercy recognizes the life in need of mercy. The person

THE SERMON

who has received healing from a merciful act knows what to say or do to be an instrument of healing in the life of the person wounded and bleeding because of life's circumstances.

Mercy and grace walk hand in hand. Mercy is the unapologetic herald of unwavering grace. When mercy is truly received, it opens the door to grace and the master plan of God in our lives; a plan that requires us to pass on that mercy and grace to those in need of it in our circle of influence.

When my co-laborer Dana Harding was young, he was involved in an incident that illustrates mercy and grace:

"A friend of mine and I were in a minor biking mishap. He received a few scrapes, bumps, and bruises, but other than that, was OK. I walked away unscathed. He went home, and since I was staying with my older cousin, I went back to my uncle's house and explained what happened. While we were planning on going down the street to make sure everything was OK, we were not expecting what happened next.

"We looked out the window, only to see a police car in their driveway! My heart fell into my sneakers. At the ripe old age of 12, I was about to be carted off to the 'big house,' the first kid in history to ever be incarcerated for illegally operating a moped. Oh, the humility!

"How could this day get any worse?

"Dad's car pulled into the driveway. Well, that answered that question!

"Dad could be a pretty gruff guy at times. A WWII veteran, a decorated Army captain, and the father of six kids—there was never a question as to where you stood with him. In twelve years of life, I had stood, looking out from inside the doghouse on more than one occasion, and it was not a place I wanted to revisit. Dad had a standing rule: Getting into trouble with any authority figure meant getting into trouble with him.

"We were quick to tell him what had happened, and he listened intently, not saying much. After all, the whole thing was just an unfortunate accident. His response was basically, 'Let's wait to see what the officer says.' Out stepped the police officer. We discussed what had happened, and he explained what laws had been broken. However, since no one was seriously injured, he let me off with a warning, and went on his way.

"However, Dad was still there; and what happened next was the biggest surprise of all. What happened next was . . . nothing.

"No yelling. No scolding. My father saw his young son, sorry for the trouble he had caused, and had mercy. He never played the just-wait-until-we-get-home card. He saw genuine remorse from his frightened child, and knew that I needed his mercy and love more than I needed to hear, yet one more time, how I had messed up. In fact, that mercy was accompanied by an act of grace. On the three-hour drive, back to our home in Maine, he pulled in to the original Brookstone store, and bought me a beautiful lock-blade pocket knife—a symbol of grace that I still own to this day."

The gift of grace is the treasure that mercy not only brings about, but never lets us forget.

Kneel scared, broken, and helpless; rise a knight.

BE BRAVE AND UPRIGHT (Unmixed Motives)

"Blessed are the pure in heart for they shall see God."

The word *pure* is derived from a Greek word that means "unfolded."

THE SERMON

When something is unfolded, it is laid bare to the beholder; nothing is hidden in the folds. It means "unmixed."

Heart is the spirit and soul of a man. It is the center of human personality. It includes the mind, the emotions, and the will. From the heart flows every decision of life. And out of the heart also flows all human misery. Matthew 15:19 says, *"For out of the heart proceed evil thoughts, murders, adulteries, fornications, thefts, false witness, blasphemies."*

If our goal as Christians is to "see God," we must live our lives as an open book, filled with integrity and the purest of motivations. If we do that, God will give us a vision of His glory, and give us the spiritual sight to see Him through the eyes of faith as long as we live on this earth (and face-to-face when we get to Heaven). However, any vision of God must be accompanied by a life that is the "real deal"—not a manufactured facade that has nothing behind it. Across the pages of Scripture, many such people saw the Lord:

- Abraham saw the Lord.

- Moses saw the Lord.

- Isaiah saw the Lord.

- Stephen saw the Lord.

- John saw the Lord.

But how could these men see God? There are some pretty significant failures in that list:

- Abraham was a liar.

- Moses was a murderer.

- John was one of the disciples who deserted Jesus in His hour of need.

Guilty as charged! However, in spite of their failures, all of these ultimately surrendered themselves to God, and lived a life of faith in Him. That is why some of these very "failures" are the same people listed as examples of faith in Hebrews 11.

In his book *The Cost of Discipleship*, Dietrich Bonhoeffer describes the pure in heart as "those whose hearts are undefiled by their own evil—and by their own virtues too."[16] He understood that, just as our evil acts can take us beyond the view of seeing the face of God, so can our own self-righteousness. In fact, Isaiah states, *"All our righteous acts are like filthy rags"* (64:6 NIV).

So, if we can't be good enough, and we can't be bad enough, how can we move closer to the Lord? I'm glad you asked. Psalm 24:4-6 declares:

> *He who has clean hands and a pure heart, who has not lifted up his soul to an idol nor sworn deceitfully.*
>
> *He shall receive blessing from the Lord and righteousness from the God of his salvation.*
>
> *This is Jacob, the generation of those who seek Him, who seek Your face. Selah!* (NIV)

In order to see the face of a friend, we have to be in the same vicinity—in the same place physically. In order so see the face of God with the eyes of faith, we must be in the same vicinity spiritually. Look at Psalm 24 again. The psalmist says the tell-tale signs of a generation that is seeking the face of God are clean hands, pure hearts, absence of idols, and commitment to truth. By taking these steps toward the presence of God, we have a promise: *"Draw near to God, and He will draw near to you"* (James 4:8). By drawing near to God in repentance, He promises to draw near to us in forgiving grace!

THE SERMON

Our life should not be a divided life. We ought to be clean, inside and out. The Pharisees in Jesus' day were guilty of being clean on the outside, but dirty, dead, and decaying on the inside.

- Is your inner life clean?

- Is your thought life holy?

- Do you lust after another person's spouse?

- Do you covet another's possessions?

- Do you secretly read or watch that which is vile?

- Do you have two (or more) different lifestyles?

In the 1950s, there was a television program called *I Led Three Lives*. It was the story of Richard Carlson, who served as a double agent for the Secret Service pretending to be someone who was the exact opposite of what he really was. There are some reading this book who live multiple lives today—right now. You have a church persona, a family persona, and a public persona. Who you are should be the same everywhere. In order to live a life that seeks (and finds) the face of God, He requires that consistent life.

In Tennyson's *King Arthur*, Sir Galahad's confession is, "My strength is the strength of ten because my heart is pure."

So, with that said:

- Kneel a liar; rise in truth.

- Kneel unfaithful; rise in integrity.

- Kneel broken and bleeding; rise with clean hands and a pure heart.

- Kneel in self-righteousness; rise in Jesus' righteousness.

- Kneel pure in heart; rise a knight!

BE WITHOUT FEAR (Unmistakable Mission)

"Blessed are the peacemakers."

Peace is the cessation of hostilities. Men and women are basically hostile—at war with self, others, and God. We live in a hostile and divided world. God sent His Son, the Prince of Peace, into the world to show us the way back to the Father. Through His sacrifice, He planted a blood-stained flag of peace, the cross, between Heaven and earth. An instrument of torture and death became the gateway to peace with God.

> *Therefore, since we have been justified through faith, we have peace with God through our Lord Jesus Christ.—* Romans 5:1 (NIV)

> *We are therefore Christ's ambassadors, as though God were making his appeal through us. We implore you on Christ's behalf: Be reconciled to God.—*2 Corinthians 5:20 (NIV)

As ambassadors of the Prince of Peace, we have the authority and obligation to offer peace to all who will trust Jesus Christ. This is the essence of soul-winning. When you set out to deliver the message of the love of Christ to another person, you are on a mission of peace. Today, in the midst of a world of bloodshed and violence, people can have inner peace that no amount of worldly conflict can take away. Our dedication to delivering this message is the mark of a child of God.

"Peacemakers . . . shall be called the children of God."

The ancient Chinese military strategist and philosopher Sun Tzu once said, "In peace prepare for war, in war prepare for peace."

As the "warrior peacekeepers" of the army of God, that is the balancing act to which we are called. Romans 16:20 says, *"The God of*

THE SERMON

peace will soon crush Satan under your feet" (NIV). In our ongoing battle with the enemy of our souls, every man, woman, or child that enters into peace with God strikes another violent blow against the enemy. The ultimate defeat of Satan and the forces of darkness will be on the heels of the restoration of peace between creation and Creator. This final, decisive blow will usher in peace for eternity.

Kneel an instrument of peace; rise a knight.

SPEAK THE TRUTH ALWAYS (Unwavering Ministry)

"Blessed are those who are persecuted for righteousness' sake."

The Uncommon Life is a blessed life, but it is also a buffeted life. Your opportunity and privilege to serve Christ will be met with opposition. Those who serve Christ will be reviled, misunderstood, abused, and ignored. In John 16, Jesus warned His disciples that to follow Him was an invitation to persecution: *"The time is coming when anyone who kills you will think they are offering a service to God"* (v. 2).

Throughout history, prophets, preachers, and believers (in general) have paid the ultimate price for their belief:

- Daniel was thrown to lions.

- Isaiah was sawn in half.

- Jeremiah was exiled.

- Stephen was stoned.

- James (the son of Zebedee) was beheaded.

- Peter was crucified.

- Paul was beheaded.

- Polycarp was burned at the stake.

RISE A KNIGHT

- John was plunged into boiling oil, then exiled to the Isle of Patmos (after the oil didn't kill him).

These, along with countless others, knew that to suffer for the cause of Christ is a countless privilege and blessing. Persecution will not stop a true believer from His duty: showing the love of Christ, exhibiting mercy, and leading others to the cross of salvation.

Nee Shu-Tsu was born in China right after the turn of the 20th century. At the age of 17, he heard the Gospel and gave his heart to Jesus. He never looked back, but spent the next thirty-two years writing, teaching, and preaching the Gospel in mainland China. He saw his role as that of the night watchman, whose job it was to awaken men to the coming of Christ. It was for that reason that he changed his name to Watchman Nee.

In 1952, Watchman Nee was imprisoned by the Communist Chinese, and spent the last 20 years of his life in confinement in prison, his only visitor being his wife. On the day of his death, he wrote, "In my sickness, I still remain joyful at heart."

When he died, a scrap of paper was found in his cell. Watchman Nee had written these words: "Christ is the Son of God who died for the redemption of sinners and was resurrected after three days. This is the greatest truth in the universe. I die because of my belief in Christ."[17]

Watchman Nee epitomized faithfulness in spite of persecution. So, why should we be surprised that the world ridicules faithful believers? You would think that a life of mercy, purity, and peace would result in favor instead of persecution.

Dietrich Bonhoeffer was a German pastor who was arrested and imprisoned by the Nazis in 1943. After his particularly brutal

THE SERMON

execution on April 9, 1945 (just 23 days before the Nazis surrendered to the Allies), the camp doctor who witnessed the event wrote:

> I saw Pastor Bonhoeffer... kneeling on the floor praying fervently to God. I was most deeply moved by the way this lovable man prayed, so devout and so certain that God heard his prayer. At the place of execution, he again said a short prayer and then climbed the few steps to the gallows, brave and composed. His death ensued after a few seconds. In the almost fifty years that I worked as a doctor, I have hardly ever seen a man die so entirely submissive to the will of God.[18]

Life is not always fair, yet this world is not the end. Consider Bonhoeffer's own words, spoken to a friend on the day before his execution: "This is the end — for me, the beginning of life." [19]

But we have hope! Matthew's words in chapter 5 continue to a conclusion in which we can take heart: *"Blessed are you when people insult you, persecute you and falsely say all kinds of evil against you because of me. Rejoice and be glad, because great is your reward in heaven, for in the same way they persecuted the prophets who were before you"* (NIV).

Our response is to maintain our joy in the Lord, whatever the consequences. Here is an Uncommon Life that is not subject to popularity in the world.

Kneel a martyr; rise a knight.

"And that is so you remember."

Daniel was swindled by his own brother. As a result, he hated him for a long time. One day, a missionary came to where Daniel lived and led him to Christ. Two years passed, and one day while walking down the street, Daniel saw his brother. Instead of the consuming anger that had gripped him years before, the love of Christ had changed him.

Daniel said, "When I saw the image of our father on his face, I had to forgive and embrace him."

As another martyr, Jim Elliot, once said, "He is no fool who gives what he cannot keep to gain that which he cannot lose."[20]

So, kneel at the foot of a blood-stained cross, having given it all for the sake of the call of Christ. Rise a knight!

THE SERMON

KEY QUESTIONS TO PONDER
Chapter 3: *Rise a Knight*

1. Give a definition of *integrity*. Now explain your definition it light of the following quote from former U.S. Senator Alan K. Simpson: "If you have integrity, nothing else matters. If you don't have integrity, nothing else matters."

2. How are we supposed to handle it when unkind words are spoken about us?

3. Discuss the following statement: Since we are trying to live as "ambassadors of peace," how can we reconcile Jesus' words to His disciples (and us) to be prepared for persecution?

"They will put you out of the synagogues; yes, the time is coming that whoever kills you will think that he offers God service" (John 16:2).

Chapter 4
IT'S A WONDERFUL LIFE
Living a Life of Lasting Influence

"You are the salt of the earth. But if the salt loses its saltiness, how can it be made salty again? It is no longer good for anything, except to be thrown out and trampled underfoot. You are the light of the world. A town built on a hill cannot be hidden. Neither do people light a lamp and put it under a bowl. Instead they put it on its stand, and it gives light to everyone in the house. In the same way, let your light shine before others, that they may see your good deeds and glorify your Father in heaven."

—Matthew 5:13-16 (NIV)

In the Christmas classic *It's A Wonderful Life*, George Bailey is the guy with stars in his eyes. George is the dreamer with his life all planned out—a life of fame, fortune, pretty women, and worldly accomplishment. He's going to design the tallest buildings. He's going to see the world. He's going to shake the dust of Bedford Falls from his feet and *be* somebody.[21]

Like the aspirations of George Bailey, the hunger for fame and stardom has swept into the upper echelons of Christianity. The bane of "celebrity" has seized many in Christian circles. Some are sacrificing

THE SERMON

Biblical standards for temporary fame and wealth. *They* are going to have the biggest and best. *They* are going to be the model to which all other ministries should aspire. *They* are going to shake the dust of the "faith of our fathers" from their feet, and be the user-friendly church that will attract the well-to-do and "beautiful" people of the 21st century. But, like shooting stars that shine brightly for a moment and then go dark, so are those who reach for human acclaim over faithfulness.

Randy Stonehill sang about his "dream of being a hero," but concluded, "Jesus is the name of the only hero I've ever found."[22]

The Uncommon Life, as we have learned . . .

- never stops hungering and growing
- gives others some slack
- is lived with integrity.

In this chapter, we discover the lasting influence of the Uncommon Life.

Leopold was an accomplished musician. In the area in which he lived, he advanced in the music community, and gained a fair amount of notoriety. However, upon the birth of his children and the years following, he began to pour himself into the lives of his children to the extent that it, quite probably, cost him in the area of personal advancement for his career. However, he continued to nurture the God-given musical talent of his children, particularly his son. Because of the self-sacrificing love of a father, Leopold may never be remembered by many for his works or accomplishments. However, his influence resounds to this day, as the world will never forget the works of his son, Wolfgang Amadeus Mozart.

The life of lasting influence, however, fights a seemingly uphill battle. It only takes watching the news for a few minutes to come to the realization that there are two incontrovertible facts we must face in life:

1. *The world is under the curse of unrelenting decay*. For all of the advances we have made throughout society (medicine, technology, etc.), particularly over the past 150 years, our planet is rotting. In Romans 3:10-18, Paul states:

> *"There is no one righteous, not even one; there is no one who understands; there is no one who seeks God.*
>
> *"All have turned away, they have together become worthless; there is no one who does good, not even one."*
>
> *"Their throats are open graves; their tongues practice deceit."*
>
> *"The poison of vipers is on their lips."*
>
> *"Their mouths are full of cursing and bitterness."*
>
> *"Their feet are swift to shed blood; ruin and misery mark their ways, and the way of peace they do not know."*
>
> *"There is no fear of God before their eyes"* (NIV).

2. *The world is engulfed in and enslaved by spiritual darkness.* All you have to do is open your eyes. On television, movies, music, and the Internet we see how spiritual darkness has permeated our society. From the courthouse to the school, to the church, the effects of an ungodly influence are there—blatant in some places and subtler in others. Philippians 2:14-16 instructs us: *"Do everything without grumbling or arguing, so that you may become blameless and pure, children of God without fault in a warped and crooked generation. Then you will shine among them like stars in the sky as you hold firmly*

THE SERMON

to the word of life. And then I will be able to boast on the day of Christ that I did not run or labor in vain" (NIV).

In spite of the darkness of His day, Jesus put His emphasis not on despair, but on hope. He looked squarely at His people and said, "Be what you are—salt and light."

Now for us, that might not sound like such a big deal. Salt is cheap, and light is everywhere and easily accessed. However, in the first century, salt and light were very valuable commodities. Jesus takes these indispensable necessities and uses them to symbolize the effects of the Kingdom citizen. He gave these people, most of whom were poor and commoners, something to aspire to. By calling them *salt* and *light*, He was establishing their inherited importance in the Kingdom of God, and their life-and-death importance to the world. When any believer's life is characterized by the Beatitudes, then he or she is salt and light in a decaying and dark world.

SALT—The Invisible Influence of the Believer

"You are the salt of the earth."

Much that is done for the glory of God is never seen by those around us. For salt to be most effective, it must lose itself in that which it is to flavor, preserve, or purify. In that same sense, believers must lose ourselves if we are to be of any use to God. When Jesus said, "You are the salt of the earth," He was throwing down the gauntlet with regard to the high esteem in which He holds His children. Calling us "salt" was a major compliment.

1. *The Worth of the Believer.* The word *salt* comes from the word *sal* or *salurus.* Our English word *salary* comes from that word. In the first century and before, salt was used as a form of payment. It

was bartered for many items including exotic woods, glass, dye, wine, and countless other items. Jesus knew the value of salt, so it was no accident that He draws that comparison. By saying, "You are salt," He is saying to all of His children, "You have great value to Me. You are precious in My sight."

2. *The Work of the Believer.* Some of the value of salt, in those days, can be attributed to its usefulness in three very specific areas: a flavoring for bland food, a preservative for meat, and a medicine for wounds.

- Salt adds flavoring. Christians should be adding flavor and spice to the world. We were never meant to be long-faced, but happy and zestful through Christ. Upon the completion of the daunting task of rebuilding the wall in Jerusalem, and in spite of the opposition, threats, and obstacles they had received in the process, Nehemiah told the people, *"The joy of the Lord is your strength."* Oliver Wendell Holmes once said, "I might have entered the ministry if certain clergymen I knew had not looked and acted so much like undertakers."[23] Christians should not be the kill-joys that the world, the secular media, and (sadly enough) we ourselves, at times, have made us out to be. We should be the ones adding flavor to life.

- Salt is a preservative. Salt has a unique quality to it that has made it a valuable preservative for centuries. When the right amount of salt is added to meat, it creates an unwelcome environment for harmful bacteria to form, while at the same time triggering the growth of beneficial bacteria, which lowers the pH levels of the meat, and speeds up the curing time. If all of these

THE SERMON

factors are working together in harmony—with salt as the catalyst—the meat is preserved, and is kept from spoiling. Properly cured meat does not even require refrigeration! What a vivid picture of the effect we as believers in Christ have on this rotting and decaying world! If we engage this culture in the proper spirit, and with the proper balance, we can have a positive, preserving, life-saving effect on the world around us. By being "in the world, but not of it," and keeping our proper perspective and focus, we can keep our society from falling into utter decay and ruin. When salt is removed from meat, the meat soon becomes rancid. When we, "the salt of the earth," are removed from this world, judgment will fall.

- The medicinal value of salt. You've heard the expression "pouring salt into an open wound." It sounds very painful, but in actuality, salt has powerful medicinal qualities. From sore throats to burns to bee stings, salt has the ability to purify and ease the discomfort of various wounds and ailments. As believers in the "Great Physician," we are to be medicinal salt—antiseptic and astringent for a sick world. Although salt has great healing properties, it stings when placed in an open wound. Even though the message we bring makes society uncomfortable, and even hostile, we dare not water down the remedy. The more watered down salt is, the less effect it has as an agent of healing. The more we water down the healing message of the cross, the less chance we have of making a real difference in this world. Jesus did not say, "You should be salt" or "You might want to consider being salt in between your pageants, politics, and programs." He said, "You *are* salt." Salt never accomplished anything in the shaker. The only way salt is of any use is if it is spent; shaken out and scattered for a desired result. In order for us to be of any use as "salt," we must be willing to be poured out—shaken out of those comfort zones commonly referred to as "pews"—and make a difference in a dull, diseased, and decaying world.

LIGHT—The Illuminating Influence of the Believer

"You are the light of the world."

Our Lord desires that His salvation, glory, and work be illuminated and visible to those in the darkness of our world. Without question, our world is in darkness. Why? Jesus explained it Himself: *"Men love darkness rather than light because their deeds are evil."* By being light in the world, we expose evil for all of its ugliness and emptiness. Darkness has no substance in and of itself. Darkness is merely the absence of light. In the presence of light, darkness has no choice but to flee. In the presence of "the Light of the world," the darkness of the enemy of our souls is dispelled, and the glory of God is revealed in full.

1. *The Source of Light.* Jesus said, *"I am the light of the world"* (John 9:5). He is pure light. Our Father is called the *"Father of lights"* (James 1:17). His light is natural. John 1:5 says, *"God is light, and in Him is no darkness at all."*

Our light is reflected light. We reflect the light of Jesus. His light shines through us. Malachi 4:2 says, *"But to you who fear My name The Sun of Righteousness shall arise With healing in His wings."* We had no light in our lives until He became the light of our lives.

THE SERMON

2. *The Shining of the Light.* Light does not try to shine. It does not stress out, strain, or struggle to illuminate its surroundings. Light just shines. However, any light that shines does so sacrificially. Any time a light is shining, it means something is being burned up. As a candle glows, the wick is slowly burned up. Every time an incandescent light is turned on, the element inside grows weaker until it burns up. Sitting in front of a cozy fireplace comes at a cost to the wood. Actually, the hotter the fire burns, the less ash is left over. The hotter we allow Jesus to burn in us, the brighter we are in the world. However, the brighter He burns, the more visible He becomes, and the less visible we are.

Are you willing to burn sacrificially so that Jesus shines brightly for all to see?

My former pastor, John Bob Riddle, had many health problems. I once heard another pastor say, "He burned the candle at both ends."

Yes, he did. And it is for that very reason that many people can now call Heaven their eternal home instead of Hell. John Bob Riddle knew the truth that light shines freely, on the shack and on the mansion. It shines on the palace and the pigsty. Every place, no matter the address, needs light. Every heart, regardless of economic or societal position, needs Christ's light.

We are commanded to let our lights shine. We are not to turn on the light, but we are to turn loose the light. If we are saved by the blood of Jesus, His light is already shining in us.

If you notice closely, hidden in this text is a list of four places our light is to shine:

- The world needs the light: "You are the light of the world."

- The city, town, and community need the light: "a city set on a hill."

- The home needs the light: "It gives light to all that are in the house."

- Individuals need the light: "Let your light so shine before men."

The message we bear is that Light. It is the Light of hope for a worn-down and hopeless world. It is the Light of help for the city that is crumbling down around us. It is the Light of aid for the failing family. It is the Light of salvation for the lost soul.

One evening, when Robert Louis Stevenson was a young boy, he was sitting at a window, watching an old man light the gas street lamps. As he sat, transfixed by the actions of the lamplighter, someone asked him what he was doing. His reply was, "I'm watching a man punch holes in the darkness."

That, my friend, is our task. We are to punch holes in the darkness of this world with the Light of the world.

Though our lives may seem insignificant and small, they are of earth-shaking importance. Yes, I believe we the church, as salt, are to pour out of the salt-shaker and shake up this planet. We are to burn and shine for Jesus in this dark world. Jesus challenged a few fishermen and ruffians in an obscure little country to impact the world. They did. I firmly believe that we, as the body of Christ, can make an impact and change the world.

It is clear that Christians are to be distinct from the surroundings. Salt and light are different: they change what they touch instead of being changed by what they encounter. To be a Christian is to be different, unusual, uncommon.

Our lives do not fit into corrupt culture. We are here to set the contrast between light and darkness; between salted and decaying;

THE SERMON

between truth and error; between wrong and right; between hope and discouragement.

But here's the catch: Both of these examples close with a warning. Salt can lose its savor, and light can be hidden under a basket. If salt loses its flavor, it gets thrown out into the street and trampled. If light is hidden, it is wasted energy and resource.

Jesus is the salt of our lives. If we lose our saltiness, then we are "good for nothing." In those days, much of the salt was not pure. If it was left stored for too long, the real salt would evaporate, leaving only a tasteless powder. If we as Christians remain inactive and stagnant in our spiritual growth and witness, we become stale and worthless. We run the risk of being "cast out and trampled under the feet of men." To put it in laymen's terms: If you lose touch with the One who adds the flavor to your life, everyone will walk all over you. Your life will be inconsequential to the Kingdom.

Light may be hidden away. The light of Jesus is displayed by good works. Work done through you to the glory of God will point men to Him. If your work is real, and done with the right motivation, while people may thank you, they will give praise to the Father for what He has done.

King Henry V of England was in a tough battle at a place called Agincourt. The chronicler Raphael Holinshed wrote about Henry after the victory had been won. "Neither would he suffer any ditties to be made and sung by the minstrels of his glorious victory, for that he would wholly have the praise and thanks altogether given to God."[24] That ought to be our purpose when serving the Lord. Don't hide the light of the Lord under a covering of pride and modesty. Allow Him to shine out of you.

Now, in the words of Clarence, "What about George Bailey?"[25]

While George had big dreams and big aspirations, he was his father's son. Every time he was faced with an opportunity to leave Bedford Falls, he was confronted with a difficult choice that would affect the lives of others, and chose to stay. Every time he had a choice between his dreams and the welfare of someone else, his dreams took a back seat. Although his father was gone, it was his father's memory that always made him choose others before himself. But in the end, he discovered that his wealth came not from owning a successful building and loan business, but from the light of lasting influence that he had on those around him—a light that came from his father's lasting influence on him.

THE SERMON

KEY QUESTIONS TO PONDER
Chapter 4: *It's A Wonderful Life*

1. Read Matthew 5:13-15. Since each believer is called to be "salt" and "light," discuss how those two elements have impacted your life.

2. In this chapter we saw salt was used for two purposes. What were they? How does that translate into our interaction with a "decaying" culture?

3. Read Matthew 5:16. If "light" is influence, then how can our light shine to influence those with whom we live, work, and go to church?

Chapter 5
BACK TO THE FUTURE
Embraces the Best of the Past

"Do not think that I have come to abolish the Law or the Prophets; I have not come to abolish them but to fulfill them. For truly I tell you, until heaven and earth disappear, not the smallest letter, not the least stroke of a pen, will by any means disappear from the Law until everything is accomplished.

Therefore anyone who sets aside one of the least of these commands and teaches others accordingly will be called least in the kingdom of heaven, but whoever practices and teaches these commands will be called great in the kingdom of heaven. For I tell you that unless your righteousness surpasses that of the Pharisees and the teachers of the law, you will certainly not enter the kingdom of heaven."

—Matthew 5:17-20 (NIV)

The past is never one's enemy; the past simply is what it is. The past can be the rope that we climb, hand-over-hand, to an Uncommon Life, or it can be the rope by which we hang ourselves on the gallows of shame, self-pity, and victimization. In every area of life, we must come to terms with the fact that, regardless of our past, it should be a

THE SERMON

prologue to a better future. There are things from the past we must take with us, as well as those things that it is in our best interest to leave behind. If we seek the face of God when dealing with our past, He will show us which are the precious gems of the past we should cling to, and which is the worthless "fool's gold" we should leave in the dust.

Author Zig Ziglar tells the story of an older native American who owned some property in Oklahoma. After many years, it was discovered there was oil on his land, instantly making him very wealthy. The man took some of his newfound wealth and decided to purchase a big car. He could often be seen driving around town, smiling and waving at people as he passed by. There was never any mistaking the old man or his car. It was the big, shiny Cadillac being pulled along by two horses. You see, no one had ever taught the old man how to put the key into the ignition to start the car.[26]

What a picture of so many lives today! How do you put the past and the future together? Do we have to harness up the horses from the past in order to pull our lives along today?

Regardless of the trappings, traditions, and turmoil of the past that we may choose to leave in the mothballs of memories, there are some things that we dare not leave behind!

One criticism of modern church life is that some have left the fundamentals of Biblical standards behind. In trying to reach people, we are told not to use words and phrases like "the cross" and "the blood," don't quote from the Scripture too much, say nothing about Hell, and do not cry out against evil. Yet, Jesus teaches us we should embrace the best of the past, as an impetus to a better future. He was "cutting-edge" in His time on this earth. He saw the perfection of Scripture not as a list of "don'ts," but as the way to real liberty. He saw faith not as fantasy, but as fulfillment. He saw abundant life not as a possibility, but as probability and promise. He saw worship as an abundant expression of pure joy.

Jesus mourned over what the religious zealots had done to the Scriptures, to the Temple, and to people who were hungry for God. Ironically, however, He was the one being attacked for His approach to Scripture, the accusation being that He was trying to abolish the Law and the Prophets. But as He states in verse 17: *"Do not think that I have come to abolish the Law or the Prophets; I have not come to abolish them, but to fulfill them."*

Religious rules were so woven into the teaching of Scripture that the religious leaders of the day would do *anything* to preserve the position and grip it gave them over the people—even commit murder.

Much like the political landscape of America, the religious landscape of Jesus' day was divided into two leadership groups: *conservative* and *liberal*. Sadducees were the liberal group of the day, denying the supernatural as well as the resurrection from the dead. Pharisees were the conservative fundamentalists. They claimed to hold to the inerrancy of Scripture.

However, what the Pharisees really held to was the inerrancy of their interpretations. The Pharisees had totally missed the divine purpose of the Law. They believed in the literal interpretation of the Law. They went as far as to actually wear the Law on their heads. Furthermore, they made the Law burdensome by adding over 5,000 pages of exceptions, instructions, and clauses. They completely majored on the externals of the Law, and completely missed the spirit of the Law. Even today in the city of Jerusalem, there are markings so that Orthodox Jews know how far they may walk on the Sabbath.

THE SERMON

But for all of their tithing, witnessing, fasting, and attending synagogue, Jesus said the Pharisees were not good enough; that their "good" didn't measure up. They failed to realize, or at least admit, that there was a righteousness that exceeded their definition. Many today feel they are Christians simply because of church membership, rituals, ordinances, and externals. Just like the Pharisees of Jesus' day, all of their good works and ideals fall far short of what God requires. This becomes crystal clear when they start looking for exceptions and ways around the rules—looking for the smallest glimmer of twisted truth or ecclesiastical loophole to support their belief that the rules don't apply to them. But Jesus issues the definitive "gotcha" to the Pharisees' maneuvering when He states, *"Unless your righteousness surpasses that of the Pharisees and the teachers of the law, you will certainly not enter the kingdom of heaven."* The righteousness of which He speaks is the righteousness that He provides, of which He is the example and the standard.

So, now the question arises: Did Jesus, in fact, abolish the Law?

CHRIST AND THE LAW

"Do not think that I have come to abolish the Law or the Prophets; I have not come to abolish them but to fulfill them."

The Law and the Prophets are both parts of the Word of God. In this passage, Jesus states He did not come to abolish them, but to fulfill them. What exactly does that mean?

- He fulfilled the prophecies of the Pentateuch (the first five books of the Old Testament).

- He fulfills the ceremonies of the Law as both priest and sacrifice.

- He fulfilled the morality of the Law by yielding Himself in perfect obedience to every precept that the Law required.

BACK TO THE FUTURE

- He paid in full the penalty of the Law, satisfying the demands of the Law with His precious blood.

Some skeptics may say, "Big deal! So, Jesus fulfilled a few ancient prophecies. It's coincidence at best."

Coincidence . . .

- that the Messiah would be born in Bethlehem? Well, that's not too hard to imagine.

- that the Messiah would be crucified? This prophecy, described in Psalm 22, was made several hundred years before crucifixion was even invented in approximately the 7th century BC.

- that the Messiah would be born of a virgin? A physical impossibility in the first century, much less at the time the prophecy was spoken.

The Old Testament contains over 300 prophecies concerning the coming Messiah (of which, Jesus fulfilled them all). In his book *Science Speaks*, Professor Peter Stoner explains that, if all of the prophecies were given the same degree of likelihood (i.e., that it was just as likely someone could be "born of a virgin" as someone could be "born in Bethlehem"), the mathematical statistical probability that one person could fulfill just eight of the Messianic prophecies is 1 in 100,000,000,000,000,000 (or 1 in 10^{17}).

Now, to explain that astronomical figure, Stoner used this scenario:

- Fill the entire State of Texas two feet deep with silver dollars (incidentally, Texas is 268,601 square miles).

- Paint one of the silver dollars red.

- Blindfold a man, and let him go anywhere in the state.

THE SERMON

The chance of that blindfolded man picking the red silver dollar on the first try is the same as one man fulfilling just eight of the Messianic prophecies of the Old Testament. Stoner goes on to state that the chance of one person fulfilling 48 prophecies is 1 in 10^{157} (an inconceivable figure). Even at 48, we're still way short of the 300-plus prophecies Jesus fulfilled![27]

By His breath, He gave the Law. By His life, He exalted the Law. By His teaching, He magnified the Law. By His death, He answered the Law's charges against us all!

In these verses in Matthew (5:17-18), Jesus threw down the gauntlet before the religious establishment of His day. Our Lord set forth the demands of the Law. Rather than "slapping religion on the back," He corrected their abuse of the ancient standard of Judaism. The same Jesus whose voice thundered out the Law on Mount Sinai to Moses answered the demands of the Law on the cross of Calvary.

THE GOOD PURPOSES OF THE LAW TODAY

1. *Eternal principles of righteousness.* In verse 18, we are told that, while heaven and earth may pass away, not one "jot or tittle" of the Law will pass away. The jot and tittle are the smallest punctuation marks in the Hebrew language. These principles, spelled out in the Law and embodied by the Lord Jesus, will continue to stand even when this planet is gone. In Luke 21:33, Jesus said: *"Heaven and earth will pass away, but my words will never pass away"* (NIV).

2. *The knowledge of sin.* Romans 6:12 gives us this charge: *"Therefore do not let sin reign in your mortal body so that you obey its evil desires"* (NIV). In any society, there must always be a standard by which people live. Without it, we would degenerate into lawlessness

and chaos. God gave us the Law to give us that standard to live by.

"What shall we say, then? Is the law sinful? Certainly not! Nevertheless, I would not have known what sin was had it not been for the law. For I would not have known what coveting really was if the law had not said, 'You shall not covet'" (Romans 7:7 NIV).

In that respect, the Law is a mirror reflecting our sinfulness. It reveals to us, not only our sin, but the penalty as well.

3. *Guardian to bring us to Christ.* Any parent that has ever filled out a school form for their child will be familiar with the term "guardian." A guardian is a person who is responsible for that child, whether by blood or adoption. A guardian is given the task of protecting the child, disciplining the child, and raising that child to be a productive member of society and obey its laws. The Law is a stern guardian that God gave us to literally discipline us toward Christ. Galatians 3:24-25 says, *"So the law was our guardian until Christ came that we might be justified by faith. Now that this faith has come, we are no longer under a guardian"* (NIV). The Law illustrates the fact that, without Jesus, we are both helpless and hopeless.

As the human embodiment of the Law, Jesus came to show us the Law was not to be a list of rules, regulations, and "hurdles" to keep us from God, but a way of righteousness—a bridge—that would lead us to God. Heaven and earth will pass away. Someday, God will "blast this cosmos to Kingdom Come."[28] But for the Christian, when that day comes, we can rest assured that we will be with Him.

THE LIFE OF THE SPIRIT

The Lord Jesus makes the transition from the external to the internal principles of the Law. When a person comes to Christ, the

THE SERMON

"Law-keeper" moves into his or her heart. Instead of being shaped and molded by the external pressure of the Law, that person becomes transformed and motivated from the inside. In Galatians 5:14, Paul tells us the entire Law can be summed up by one phrase or act: *"Love your neighbor as yourself"* (NIV).

What is it that drives people to love their neighbors as themselves? For the answer to that, we must answer the question, Who is my neighbor?

- A Sunday school teacher named Edward Kimball considered a young man named Dwight to be his neighbor. Dwight L. Moody considered the people of Chicago to be his.

- Missionary Jim Elliot considered a Huaorani tribe in Ecuador to be his neighbors. His wife, Elisabeth, considered them the same, even after they killed her husband.

- Evangelist Mordecai Ham considered a young man named William to be his neighbor. William (Billy) Graham befriended the people of the world.

Through the power of the indwelling love of Christ, our neighbor becomes anyone we come into contact with, regardless of age, race, gender, or social standing. In and of ourselves, we do not have the ability to maintain that level of commitment to reaching out to the world around us. Our righteousness just doesn't measure up: *"All of us have become like one who is unclean, and all our righteous acts are like filthy rags; we all shrivel up like a leaf, and like the wind our sins sweep us away"* (Isaiah 64:6 NIV).

Yet, by the simple act of trusting Christ, we no longer have to rely on our righteousness to give us the spiritual endurance to carry out His commands. Second Corinthians 5:21 tells us God made Him who had no sin to be sin for us, so that in Him we might become the righteousness of God. By accepting what Jesus did on the cross and by His blood, His righteousness becomes our righteousness!

> *But now apart from the law the righteousness of God has been made known, to which the Law and the Prophets testify. This righteousness is given through faith in Jesus Christ to all who believe. There is no difference between Jew and Gentile, for all have sinned and fall short of the glory of God, and all are justified freely by His grace through the redemption that came by Christ Jesus. God presented Christ as a sacrifice of atonement, through the shedding of His blood—to be received by faith. He did this to demonstrate His righteousness, because in His forbearance He had left the sins committed beforehand unpunished— He did it to demonstrate His righteousness at the present time, so as to be just and the one who justifies those who have faith in Jesus* (Romans 3:21-26 NIV).

In his letter to the Christians in Rome, Paul is stating that, not only has the righteousness of God become a reality through the life, death, and resurrection of Jesus, but that both the Law and the Prophets testify to that fact. If the Jewish people of the day had truly understood the spirit of the Law, and embraced their past and their prophets, they would have seen Jesus for who He really was. But like so many people today, they allowed the gift to slip through their fingers.

> *For if, by the trespass of the one man, death reigned through that one man, how much more will those who receive God's abundant provision of grace and of the gift of righteousness reign in life through the one man, Jesus Christ! Consequently, just as one trespass resulted in*

> condemnation for all people, so also one righteous act
> resulted in justification and life for all people. For just
> as through the disobedience of the one man the many
> were made sinners, so also through the obedience of
> the one man the many will be made righteous (Romans
> 5:17-19 NIV).

However, for those who have accepted Christ, the righteous One, we do not keep the Law in order to be saved. The reality is that the Law-giver and Law keeper lives His life through us. The following verses set forth the life the Holy Spirit lives through us. These standards are not some new set of rules to live up to. Rather, they are the life of the Lord Jesus.

"Dear children, do not let anyone lead you astray. The one who does what is right is righteous, just as he is righteous" (1 John 3:7 NIV). Righteousness is the life of Jesus flowing out of you. It cannot be earned or achieved through good works, piety, or penitence. It is the by-product of the heart that seeks after the face of God.

"But seek first the kingdom of God and His righteousness, and all these things shall be added to you" (Matthew 6:33). When you bow before Him as King, then you receive His life in exchange for your old life.

"He himself bore our sins in his body on the tree, so that we might die to sins and live for righteousness; by his wounds you have been healed" (1 Peter 2:24 NIV).

> Brothers, think of what you were when you were called.
> Not many of you were wise by human standards; not
> many were influential; not many were of noble birth. But
> God chose the foolish things of the world to shame the
> wise; God chose the weak things of the world to shame

> *the strong. God chose the lowly things of this world and the despised things—and the things that are not—to nullify the things that are, so that no one may boast before him. It is because of him that you are in Christ Jesus, who has become for us wisdom from God—that is, our righteousness, holiness and redemption. Therefore, as it is written: "Let the one who boasts boast in the Lord"* (1 Corinthians 1:26-31 NIV).

So, what of your past? Maybe you made some foolish mistakes. Maybe you lost your influence because of wrong choices. Maybe you were born on the wrong side of the tracks. As I said at the beginning of this chapter, the past is what it is. However, by embracing His past—a past filled with righteousness, peace, joy, and hope for the future—He will give you the wisdom to know what past to cling to . . . and what past to leave in the past.

THE SERMON

KEY QUESTIONS TO PONDER
Chapter 5: *Back to the Future*

1. Read Matthew 5:17-18. Jesus states He did not come to abolish the Law, but to fulfill the Law. What does that mean for us today? How did He fulfill the Law?

2. Read Galatians 3:24-25. It states the Law is a guardian given to show us that without Christ we are helpless and hopeless.

- True or false? The Law of God is a mirror reflecting our sinfulness.

- True or false? We can be saved by keeping the Law.

Back up your answers with Scripture.

3. Has the modern church strayed from the fundamentals of Biblical standards? Have we allowed human traditions to replace the Word of God? Discuss with an objective view.

Chapter 6
HEROES
Life Lived from the Inside Out

"You have heard that it was said to the people long ago, 'You shall not murder, and anyone who murders will be subject to judgment.' But I tell you that anyone who is angry with a brother or sister will be subject to judgment. Again, anyone who says to a brother or sister, 'Raca,' is answerable to the court. And anyone who says, 'You fool!' will be in danger of the fire of hell.

Therefore, if you are offering your gift at the altar and there remember that your brother or sister has something against you, leave your gift there in front of the altar. First go and be reconciled to them; then come and offer your gift. Settle matters quickly with your adversary who is taking you to court. Do it while you are still together on the way, or your adversary may hand you over to the judge, and the judge may hand you over to the officer, and you may be thrown into prison. Truly I tell you, you will not get out until you have paid the last penny.

You have heard that it was said, 'You shall not commit adultery.' But I tell you that anyone who looks at a woman lustfully has already committed adultery

THE SERMON

with her in his heart. If your right eye causes you to stumble, gouge it out and throw it away. It is better for you to lose one part of your body than for your whole body to be thrown into hell. And if your right hand causes you to stumble, cut it off and throw it away. It is better for you to lose one part of your body than for your whole body to go into hell."

—Matthew 5:21-30 (NIV)

In the HBO Documentary *Profiles of the Pacific,* Chuck Tatum shared this story. As a survivor of The Battle of Iwo Jima during World War II, he was once asked by a small boy if he was a "hero of Iwo Jima." Mr. Tatum replied, "No, son, I'm only a survivor. We buried all the heroes."[29]

Now, contrast the humility of Mr. Tatum with this attitude: "I want to be a member of your church. I tithe off the gross, I'm here every time the doors are open, and I fast twice a week. I don't smoke, drink, or chew (or run with girls who do)."

Wow! How impressive is that? Most churches would knock themselves out to fill their pews with people like this—people whose external lives were so remarkable and above reproach. I mean, what can you say about someone who has it so together—so perfect and so proper in their appearance?

Jesus had a term He used to describe such people: "whitewashed tombs." The fundamentalists of Jesus' day were the Pharisees. They believed in the Old Testament. They believed in life after death. They believed in the resurrection of the dead. When it came to the externals of the Law, they crossed every "t" and dotted every "i."

Yet, in spite of their impressive lifestyle, piety, and "perfection," they were tragically deceived and lost.

In Matthew 23 (starting at verse 13), Jesus issues a stinging indictment against the Pharisees. *"Woe to you"* is a phrase Jesus uses seven times between verse 13 and the end of the chapter. In verse 27, He says, *"Woe to you, teachers of the law and Pharisees, you hypocrites! You are like whitewashed tombs, which look beautiful on the outside, but on the inside are full of the bones of the dead and everything unclean"* (NIV).

At this point, I probably need to clarify one thing. For the Christian, the issue of external appearance is a double-edged sword. Just as one can go too far focusing on "looking like a Christian" (legalism), there is also a school of thought that says that, in order to reach the world, we must dress, act, and talk like the world. Paul said, *"I have become all things to all people so that by all possible means I might save some"* (1 Corinthians 9:22 NIV).

However, in the verses before, Paul makes it plain that, although he may reach out to a person and meet them at their level, he does so without crossing any moral boundaries set up by God ("To those under the Law I became *like* one under the Law though I myself am not under the Law"), so as to win those under the Law. To those not having the Law, he became *like* one not having the Law ("though I am not free from God's law but am under Christ's law"), so as to win those not having the Law.

Finding a common ground on which to begin a dialogue with the world is one thing; compromising our core beliefs, morals, and conscience in the interest of looking "cool" to the new generation is dangerous territory. The result can mean losing your witness, not just to the generation you are trying to reach, but to older and future generations as well.

THE SERMON

While externals are not without importance, we cannot be driven by externals only. As Christians, we believe what is in the heart and what flows from the heart is what really counts. First Samuel 16:7 says, *"The Lord does not look at the things people look at. People look at the outward appearance, but the Lord looks at the heart"* (NIV).

What made the Pharisees so deceived was their own interpretation of the rules. The Pharisees wrote the *Mishna*, which was a commentary on the Scripture and Law. Later, they wrote the six sedarim (also known as *Gemara*), which was a commentary on the *Mishna*. However, in time the Pharisees and Rabbis came to value their interpretation and application above that of Scripture. An accepted school of thought in Talmudic teaching was, "The Bible is like water, the *Mishna* like wine, and the six sedarim (*Gemara*) like sweet wine: none of which can the world be without."

In many cases, Scripture was manipulated and distorted into something that they could use to justify their own passions and lusts. The *Mishna* and *Gemara* became vehicles whereby these men could "legally" divorce their wives so they could marry younger women. It made it possible for them to forsake the Law's direction regarding caring for their aging parents, by using the "law of *corban*" (that which is dedicated to God) to rob their parents and pad their own pockets. In essence, they would steal from their parents and use that money on themselves for "religious purposes." Furthermore, it absolved them from showing mercy toward sinners (at their own discretion). Think about the woman who was caught in adultery (John 8). Where was the man?

But Jesus made no bones about taking on their man-made rules. Notice the formula He uses throughout Matthew 5: *"You have heard it said . . . yet I say."*

Through the simple use of this phrase, Jesus is subtly revealing that He is God. He has come to scrape away what has been placed on the Holy Law, and to show that it is the heart motive that counts. He shows us that real faith flows from the heart—from the inside out! Holiness of life is not an emotion but a choice. When you come to Christ, you get the Ruler, not just the rules. God gives us the power to choose what is right, and that choice is born from the faith that is in our hearts.

"Pride goes before destruction, a haughty spirit before a fall" (Proverbs 16:18 NIV).

"So, if you think you are standing firm, be careful that you don't fall! No temptation has overtaken you except what is common to mankind. And God is faithful; he will not let you be tempted beyond what you can bear. But when you are tempted, he will also provide a way out so that you can endure it" (1 Corinthians 10:12-13 NIV).

Any one of us can fall into the trap the Pharisees fell into—pride. At the time we begin to impress ourselves with how well we are doing living this Christian life, that is when we should be most on our guard. We are nothing without His grace and His mercy. We must always be cognizant of the fact that all of our righteousness (apart from Him) is garbage—filthy rags. Remembering that will keep us from falling into the temptation from which all others are born. Remember, "original sin" was not Adam and Eve eating the fruit in the garden. The original sin was the pride of Lucifer that said, *"I will make myself like the Most High"* (Isaiah 14:14 NIV). However, God will *always* give us a way of escape, no matter how strong the temptation. He provides the escape hatch; it is up to us to use it.

Now, let's look at life from the inside out. Here our Lord deals with the root causes of external evil. Here is when we need the Spirit of Christ to help us.

THE SERMON

CONTROL MY TEMPER.

"But I tell you that anyone who is angry with a brother or sister will be subject to judgment."

How often are we angry, even with those in our own church family? The letter of the Law was, in the Pharisees' understanding, "anything goes as long as you do not kill." However, Jesus reveals that murder goes beyond the act of physically killing another person. He points out three ways we commit murder without lifting a finger:

1. *Rage.* You consider a person to be dead to you because you cannot forgive them. The problem with this, however, is that the person most affected by your inability to forgive is *you*! The ancient Roman philosopher Lucius Annaeus Seneca once described anger in this way: "Anger—an acid that can do more harm to the vessel in which it is stored than to anything on which it is poured." Living a life of carrying a grudge against another person can lead to any number of physical ailments, including high blood pressure, ulcers, hypertension, and cardiac issues.

2. *Ridicule.* You can murder another person's self-esteem. By speaking words of ridicule and condemnation, you can kill the spirit of another person. When a person calls another person a "good-for-nothing fool," he is speaking a curse against one who is made in the image of God.

3. *Reputation.* Words spoken in an attempt to tear down a person in the eyes of others, minimizing them in the minds of their friends and colleagues, is another form of murder. Of the three forms we have discussed, this can also be the most damaging in that the poison of negativity is spread into the minds of others, and the damage is not contained between two individuals. While amends can be made

between two people with just a few words, it is much more difficult to repair the wide-spread damage done to a person's reputation.

DO NOT BE A CHURCH PHONY.

"First go and be reconciled to them; then come and offer your gift."

In the movie *Kingdom of Heaven*, while rallying the people of Jerusalem prior to the onslaught by the army of Saladin, Balian of Ibelin makes this statement: "We fight over an offense we did not give, against those who were not alive to be offended."

Sounds like a lot of people in the church of Jesus Christ today. We get offended over the smallest things, then wear that offense like some kind of badge of honor. Worst of all, we take up the offense of someone else, over an issue that we are neither a part of, or have a clear understanding of. We refuse to be the one to cross the "picket-line of pride," and subsequently block the blessing of God. We keep God's best from falling on our own lives, and short-change what God may want to do in the lives of others through us.

A friend of mine shared this story with me:

"I was serving in a church when I came to be at odds with another prominent member of the congregation. Our disagreement resulted in an offense that led me to withdraw from most events and opportunities in the church that would put us into contact with each other. This went on for over two years, until finally one day (the Lord had so convicted me about it), I decided that I was going to apologize to this person the next time I saw him (if for no other reason, then just for not loving him the way I should).

"However, before I saw him to apologize, I received a phone call. It was this man, calling me to see if we could meet and talk. I agreed,

THE SERMON

and the next day, he showed up at my place of business. We sat in my office, talked, laughed, cried, and made amends for the wasted years.

"We immediately began working together on some projects for the church, and when we did, something amazing happened: Other relationships began to be reconciled, new bridges and opportunities were created with regard to ministry, and the 'dark cloud' seemed to lift from the things I was involved in. There was freedom in my worship that I had not experienced in a long time, and by working together, we were finding that we could accomplish much more for the Kingdom than trying to do it on our own. This brother went on to become, not just an effective co-laborer for Christ, but a good friend as well."

The Apostle John summed it up pretty well when he wrote: *"If anyone says, 'I love God,' and hates his brother, he is a liar; for he who does not love his brother whom he has seen, how can he love God, whom he has not seen?"* (1 John 4:20).

Your church giving or service cannot take the place of bad relationships. Make getting right with your fellow believer a priority over religious activity.

LEARN THE POWER OF AGREEMENT OVER ANGER.

"Settle matters quickly with your adversary who is taking you to court."

In the legal profession, you often hear the phrase "settled out of court." Often times, this is a situation where one or both parties realize the truth of this verse: It is better to settle a dispute before going before a judge who is impartial, indifferent, and bound by law and precedent. While you may not actually go to jail, by the time the judge finishes ruling against you, you might wish you had. Furthermore, when a dispute is settled out of court, the record is often sealed, and the specifics of the case never go public.

The warning in this verse is twofold. First, there are earthly consequences when we allow our conflicts to go public—humiliation, fines, penalties, and loss of future opportunities are just a few. The alternative is so much easier: If you are wrong, agree and apologize. If you are right, forgive and let it go.

Second, when we fail to forgive, God becomes our adversary. Our failure to let someone else "off the hook" for an offense puts us squarely in the sights of God for our own offenses. Jesus said in Matthew 6:15: *"But if you do not forgive others their sins, your Father will not forgive your sins."*

In the parable of the unforgiving servant, Jesus paints a graphic picture of the repercussions of our unforgiveness: *"Then the master called the servant in. 'You wicked servant,' he said, 'I canceled all that debt of yours because you begged me to. Shouldn't you have had mercy on your fellow servant just as I had on you?' In anger his master handed him over to the jailers to be tortured, until he should pay back all he owed"* (Matthew 18:32-34 NIV).

However, if we choose to forgive and walk in love, Jesus paints an entirely different picture, just a few verses before: *"Again, truly I tell you that if two of you on earth agree about anything they ask for, it will be done for them by my Father in heaven. For where two or three gather in my name, there am I with them"* (vv. 19-20 NIV).

KEEP MY SECRET LIFE CLEAN.

"But I tell you that anyone who looks at a woman lustfully has already committed adultery with her in his heart."

THE SERMON

In today's society, we are inundated with the sensual and the sexual. Everywhere you turn, sex is used to sell almost everything you can imagine, and while accidentally stumbling upon or viewing such an image is not a sin, staying and dwelling on it is. With the advent of the Internet, pornography and perversion that was once thought of as confined to the recesses of shady places and dark alleys are now readily available in our own homes. The online site *EnoughIsEnough* shared these statistics about the pornography industry:

- More than four in ten Americans now say pornography is morally acceptable.

- Every minute, nearly 64,000 new visitors arrive at a porn site.

- Every second, 962 Internet users are typing adult search terms into search engines.

- Every minute; 12 new pornographic videos are being uploaded.[30]

In this scripture, Jesus traces the problem of sin—especially the sins of the flesh—to the source. It all begins with lust or desire, and once that initial, unchecked temptation turns into daydreaming and fantasizing, sin is at the door—luggage in tow and ready to move in.

James recognized this when he said: *"When tempted, no one should say, 'God is tempting me.' For God cannot be tempted by evil, nor does he tempt anyone; but each person is tempted when they are dragged away by their own evil desire and enticed. Then, after desire has conceived, it gives birth to sin; and sin, when it is full-grown, gives birth to death"* (James 1:13-15 NIV).

In this passage, James gives us the progression: Lust leads to conception; conception leads to sin; sin leads to death. The graveyard of broken homes and lives is filled with epitaphs that read like a dime-store novel:

HEROES

- The "harmlessness" of viewing online porn when no one was watching
- The "innocent" conversation, born out of the boredom and loneliness of frequent business trips
- The "accidental" one-night stand
- The lies and deception that accompany the years-long affair
- The pain and devastation of a family torn apart because of one person's "harmless" actions.

Jesus draws a sobering illustration when He says that, if what we see with our right eye causes us to sin, it would be better to go blind than to go to Hell. If what we do with our hand causes us to stumble, it would be better to lose it and be physically challenged than to spend eternity in torment, separated from God.

Finally, let me ask you a question: What is your definition of a hero? Is it someone who does the unexpected or the unexplained? Is it someone who does something most would consider uncommon? The interesting thing about someone who does something that most people would deem as "heroic" is that, while it may seem like a sudden, impulsive act of bravery, I would venture to say it is something about that person's inherent quality that pushed them to do the extraordinary. In other words, if it wasn't there to begin with, it isn't going to suddenly come to the surface in a time of crisis. It is something that is inside of them to start with, but becomes apparent when called upon. It is a quality that is uncommon.

Former tennis great Arthur Ashe once said, *"True heroism is remarkably sober, very undramatic. It is not the urge to surpass all others at whatever the cost, but the urge to serve others at whatever the cost."*[31] Living a life from the inside out is living a life of service. It's about living a life of integrity when no one is applauding, and a life of holiness when no one is watching.

THE SERMON

Twice in Matthew 5, Jesus warns us about Hell. In verses 22 and 30, He makes it very clear that our actions have consequences, and that sin is the key that throws open the gates of the path to Hell. In the mind of Jesus, sin is serious business.

However, Jesus took all of that for us. He loved us so much that He took the torments of Hell upon Himself to give us a way of escape. It should impress us, to the point of speechless wonder and humility, that God went to the lengths that He went to save each and every one of us from the death and eternal punishment we deserved.

So, while every hero in history has eventually been buried, Jesus is the only One who got back up. He rose from the grave to set an example that we can follow, to live a life that is singular in purpose, from a deep-seated desire for the things of God.

KEY QUESTIONS TO PONDER
Chapter 6: *Heroes*

1. Read Matthew 23. Who were the Pharisees? Why did Jesus call them "whitewashed tombs"?

2. Have you had difficulty in controlling anger toward those who have hurt and betrayed you? How have you sought to retaliate against those you deem enemies? Discuss, but don't use names.

3. Do you have any attitudes (internal) or actions (external) that need to be repented of? Are you willing to love your enemies as Jesus loved His? If not, why not?

Chapter 7

PROMISES, PROMISES

The Life that Keeps Its Promises

"It has been said, 'Anyone who divorces his wife must give her a certificate of divorce.' But I tell you that anyone who divorces his wife, except for sexual immorality, makes her the victim of adultery, and anyone who marries a divorced woman commits adultery.

Again, you have heard that it was said to the people long ago, 'Do not break your oath, but fulfill to the Lord the vows you have made.' But I tell you, do not swear an oath at all: either by heaven, for it is God's throne; or by the earth, for it is his footstool; or by Jerusalem, for it is the city of the Great King. And do not swear by your head, for you cannot make even one hair white or black. All you need to say is simply 'Yes' or 'No'; anything beyond this comes from the evil one."

—Matthew 5:31-37 (NIV)

After the Beatitudes, Jesus gives us seven clear paragraphs of commandments. In his massive two-volume commentary on Matthew, F. D. Bruner espoused the belief that these commandments correspond to the days of the week:

THE SERMON

Sunday (5:17-20): Biblical Piety Day

Monday (5:21-26): Mercy Day

Tuesday (5:27-30): Sexual Purity Day

Wednesday (5:31-32): Marital Fidelity Day

Thursday (5:33-37): Truth Day

Friday (5:38-42): Peacemaking Day

Saturday (5:43-48): Love Your Enemy Day [32]

It could be that in the early church, children memorized and recited these commands on their respective days. For the purposes of this chapter, we will look at the Wednesday and Thursday commandments, both of which deal with the issue of keeping our promises.

For those of us who grew up raised by members of "The Greatest Generation"—the generation of people who survived the Great Depression, then went on to fight in World War II—the phrase "a man's word is his bond" resonates as a part of the collective mentality. However, with the advent of the cultural revolution that began during the 1960s, and the self-indulgence that came with it, moral traits like modesty, decency, and propriety became subjective to the standard of the masses, and honesty became a casualty of the revolution.

As evidenced by what we see in the news with regard to the divorce rate, business deals gone bad, as well as broken contracts and treaties on the national and world stages, it seems that the current mentality of society can now be summed up in the 1983 song by the rock band Naked Eyes which includes these lines: "You made me promises, promises you knew you'd never keep." [33]

Instead of "a man's word is his bond," it seems that "promises were made to be broken" has become the mantra of the day. Where it used to be an affront if a person broke their word, it is now merely a pleasant surprise if someone keeps it. We see this in the vows made in marriage ceremonies, courtrooms, New Year's resolutions, and political campaigns. As soon as the prettier woman, better business deal, more convenient social position, or big-money special interest comes along, what was a binding agreement in the sight of God becomes something that "seemed like a good idea at the time."

Jesus emphasized in this teaching the importance of keeping our promises. Some of the greatest disappointments in life revolve around people who name the name of Christ failing to keep their word. In this passage, Jesus deals with two areas of promise-keeping: the marriage vow, and the act of keeping one's word.

THE MARRIAGE PROMISE

"Anyone who divorces his wife, except for sexual immorality, makes her the victim of adultery, and anyone who marries a divorced woman commits adultery."

The purpose of this word is to protect exploited women from the male misogamist. The religious teachers around Jesus' day were the rabbis Hillel, Shammai, and later, Akiba. They interpreted the Mosaic Law of Deuteronomy 24 differently. Deuteronomy 24 commands the man to give his wife a "bill of divorcement." In putting away his wife, a husband was at least supposed to give her the dignity of a document indicating that the decision was not hers, but his. Furthermore, the document was to indicate the cause for his decision.

THE SERMON

However, according to Rabbi Hillel, the law for divorce was not limited to sexual infidelity, but could also be issued for bad cooking or unacceptable housekeeping. Rabbi Shammai stated that the law of divorce was limited to sexual infidelity. Rabbi Akiba said if a man no longer found his wife attractive, and found someone else, divorce was acceptable.

As you can see, in the teachings of these rabbis, the woman is being marginalized. Their interpretation of Scripture created the "disposable woman." This was male chauvinism at its absolute worst. Men were not only dumping their wives for a "newer model"; they were not giving them a written cause. Therefore, it was assumed they were sexually impure. Subsequently, if the woman remarried, she and her new husband were called "adulterers."

The Greek text of Matthew 5:32 is translated by Dr. Bruner as follows: *"But I say to you that any man divorcing his wife for any other reason than sexual infidelity drives her into adultery."*

In His teaching, Jesus is saying the act of sexual infidelity was, in and of itself, a divorce. I have spent years doing marriage counseling, and can say unequivocally that the only thing harder than divorce is marriage. Making a marriage work is tough business. In today's culture of blaming everyone else, it's much easier to blame our spouse when something goes wrong, when the spark is gone, or when happiness has been relegated to mere existence.

However, this is where the subjects of honesty and promises come in. For most of us, our marriage vows were about providing for the needs of the other person – "to love, honor, and cherish you until death do us part." I cannot imagine a person agreeing to a vow that states, "I promise to love you and stay faithful to you as long as you make me

PROMISES, PROMISES

happy (according to my definition of *happiness*), meet my needs, keep me entertained, and don't cross me."

On the contrary, the reality of the promise hits homes when . . .

- the wife of an unfaithful husband chooses to honor her vows and stay, even though he didn't honor his.

- the diagnosis is Alzheimer's, and the decision is to stay and care for the afflicted spouse to the very end.

- although we have grown apart, we make a conscious decision to stay and work it out, even though running away seems easier.

Marriage can be tough, but anything valuable and precious in life is worth fighting for. Working through the difficulties of marriage has more than its share of headaches, but the rewards of a successful marriage are worth any hardship we may endure.

An old preacher was once telling his congregation that it was he and his wife's anniversary. "Today is our anniversary!" he exclaimed to his parishioners. "We have been happily married for 27 years!"

The crowd applauded. "And that's not too bad out of 35," he added with a chuckle.

Whether kidding or not, this preacher understood the principle of "for better or for worse." In this humorous way, he made it clear that, while marriage is not always a picnic, making the decision to stay during the hard times makes the commitment that much sweeter. What seems like "not much of a picnic," over time, can become a savory banquet of friendship, love, and intimacy.

There is nothing uncommon about making up the rules as we go along. There is nothing special about living a life set to the standard of "self." There is nothing remarkable about constantly changing our

THE SERMON

goals to accommodate our shortcomings. When God set the laws of nature in place, He didn't consult a group of scientists or Greenpeace. When He etched the Ten Commandments into the stone tablets, He didn't ask Moses, "Do these sound OK to you?" When He created the laws by which we as a society relate to each other (authority, government, business, church, etc.), there are some principles that are not subject to interpretation; they are simply truth. The area of marriage and divorce is no exception:

- God's ideal for marriage is one man and one woman for life.
- There are casualties in every divorce. All divorces cause hurt, damage, and sin.
- There are three legitimate grounds for divorce: sexual infidelity, physical abandonment (1 Corinthians 7:10-16), and abuse. In the case of abuse where a spouse and children are in danger, the divorce actually becomes an act of faith.
- Divorce should always be a last alternative. The counsel of the messages of Jesus is about loving our enemies, as well as forgiveness. Looking through the glasses of these two topics brings this issue into sharp focus. Every effort must be made to salvage a marriage that is in trouble. A life lived at the foot of the cross of Jesus means that such a marriage has a chance of surviving, just as long as both parties are willing to die to self.
- When a third party becomes involved in the fray of a battleground marriage, they are no longer considered innocent bystanders. Any individual who enters into a relationship with a married person is contributing to dissolution of a covenant made before God. Such an individual will be held accountable for their participation in tearing down "what God has joined together."

However, while God makes it very clear in His word how much He hates divorce, He makes it equally clear that He stands ready to love and save the repentant (and even remarried) divorcee. While Jesus clearly stands ready to protect the exploited casualty of any divorce, He also desires to forgive and restore those whose marriages have failed due to their own actions. It is the church's responsibility, as the earthly representatives of Christ, to be agents of restoration and forgiveness for those whose marriages have failed.

SPEAKING THE TRUTH

"The greatest single cause of atheism in the world today is Christians who acknowledge Jesus with their lips, and walk out the door and deny Him by their lifestyle. This is what an unbelieving world simply finds unbelievable."—Brennan Manning

The truth that we speak with our lips is the truth that we must reflect with our lifestyle. To the generation that is rising in our culture today, honesty is at the top of the list of what they hold sacred. They listen to what we say, and they watch the way we conduct ourselves. If those two things do not match, they discard our message as irrelevant, hypocritical, and phony.

Jesus' teaching in Matthew 5:33-37 seeks to protect speech in the same way the previous command protects sex. These verses may be summarized in the following ways:

1. *Speak faithfully.* Keep your promises to God and before God. *"Again, you have heard that it was said to the people long ago, 'Do not break your oath, but fulfill to the Lord the vows you have made'"* (v. 33 NIV).

THE SERMON

Obviously, oaths are not sin, but are a necessity in any civil society. We see it all of the time: from courtrooms and classrooms (the Pledge of Allegiance) to swearing in political figures. We take oaths as a way of saying, "I will speak the truth. I will abide by the rules. I will do my best to uphold, with integrity, the position I am taking." When people are bound by an oath, then act in a manner unbecoming of their office (as in politics), when disciplinary action is taken, it is not just about a wrong that was committed; it is (in many cases) equally about the violation of the oath that they took.

Judges 11 tells the story of Jephthah. He led the Israelites from the region of Gilead into battle against the Ammonites. At the beginning of the battle, Jephthah made a vow to the Lord: *If you give the Ammonites into my hands, whatever comes out of the door of my house to meet me when I return in triumph from the Ammonites will be the Lord's, and I will sacrifice it as a burnt offering*" (v. 30-31).

At the conclusion of the battle, when the Ammonites were defeated, Jephthah returned home in triumph, only to be greeted by his only child, his daughter, who came dancing out of the door to meet him. Jephthah was distraught when he realized what he had done, but knew that his vow, no matter how rash, had been made before God, must be kept. Furthermore, he had so instilled in his daughter the necessity of honoring vows made to the Lord that she never asked to be spared: *"'My father,' she replied, 'you have given your word to the Lord. Do to me just as you promised, now that the Lord has avenged you of your enemies, the Ammonites'"* (v. 36).

This extreme example, illustrates the point that vows made to God must be taken with the utmost seriousness and sincerity. While we do live in an age of grace, we must never be flippant when making vows before a Holy God.

PROMISES, PROMISES

2. *Speak honestly.* Truth without exaggeration and not needing explanation. *"But I tell you, do not swear an oath at all: either by heaven, for it is God's throne; or by the earth, for it is his footstool; or by Jerusalem, for it is the city of the Great King. And do not swear by your head, for you cannot make even one hair white or black"* (vv. 34-36 NIV).

We often hear people use the phrase "I swear," seemingly as a way to get their point across. But why is it that we seem to think we need such a strong qualifier when trying to get people to believe what we are saying? Could it be that we have lived a life in such a way as to not inspire confidence in simple assurances? Ouch!

In these verses, Jesus is making the point that exaggerated phrases, in order to prove that one is truthful, are unnecessary. A person's words should be so honest across the years that loud and forceful explanations of proof are not needed.

3. *Speak clearly.* Truth that is not subject to interpretation. *"All you need to say is simply 'Yes' or 'No'; anything beyond this comes from the evil one"* (v. 37 NIV).

All of us who lived during the Clinton Administration have probably at one time or another seen the clips of President Clinton during his grand-jury testimony. Here are some of his interesting quotes from the proceeding:

"It depends on what the meaning of the word *is* is."

"It depends on how you define *alone*. . . ."

"There were a lot of times when we were alone, but I never really thought we were."

THE SERMON

After going on national television and adamantly denying charges of sexual misconduct, President Clinton was forced to finally admit that he was not just guilty, but that he had "misled" the nation. However, this scandal was just one in a long line of political controversies that date back for centuries. So many politicians use rhetoric to disguise an unwillingness to take a stand. However, truth is not just about those in the public-service arena. So many times, people bend the truth to the breaking point, and claim that what they are saying is truth, "depending on your point of view." But when we speak, it should not be with double talk and certain vantage points in mind. If something has to be seen from a certain, narrow perspective in order to be perceived as truth, there is probably little truth to be found. What we find in verse 37 is a call to trustworthiness and integrity.

Ken Hartley, the worship leader at our church, conveyed this story. When he was about 5 years old, he was caught in lies on several different occasions. Every time, his father would give him a spanking. One day, he was being disrespectful to his mother, and was sent to his room to await his father's return. When his father got home, he went in to face his young son. Ken told his father he didn't want to be spanked, and after some discussion, his father assured him that he would not spank him this time, in spite of how disappointed he was in his young son.

As Ken rose to leave the room, he had just reached the door when, all of a sudden, he felt a hard, painful lash across his rear end. With tears in his eyes, he turned to face his father, who was standing over him. As he looked into his father's face, he heard the words that he never forgot: "It hurts to be lied to, doesn't it?"

PROMISES, PROMISES

> *"I never forgot that lesson," said Ken. He learned the lesson of these verses at a very early age. He learned that, when we are dishonest and untrustworthy, it not only becomes a painful experience for us, but it hurts the heart of the Father as well.*[34]

It's a matter of trust. When we make a promise, we are making it before God, and any promise made before God *must* be kept.

I remember promising my daughter that I would take pictures of her pep squad when she was in middle school. When the time for the event came, I never showed up. Over time, I began to notice that her attitude toward me changed. Years later, after she had entered college, she told me how hurt she was that I had failed to keep my promise on that specific occasion.

- Broken promises lead to broken trust.
- Broken trust leads to broken people.
- Broken people lead to broken lives.

THE SERMON

KEY QUESTIONS TO PONDER
Chapter 7: *Promises, Promises*

1. Read Matthew 5:33-37. Do you agree that instead of "A man's word is his bond," it seems the mantra of the day is, "Promises were made to be broken"?

2. Read the story of Jephthah in Judges 11. Did Jephthah make in mistake in keeping his vow to the Lord? What do you think of his daughter's response in verse 36?

3. Why is important to "never make a promise you don't intend to keep"? Can you think of any examples from your life experience that back up that statement?

Chapter 8
GREAT EXPECTATIONS
Goes Beyond what Is Expected

"You have heard that it was said, 'Eye for eye, and tooth for tooth'. But I tell you, do not resist an evil person. If anyone slaps you on the right cheek, turn to them the other cheek also. And if anyone wants to sue you and take your shirt, hand over your coat as well. If anyone forces you to go one mile, go with them two miles. Give to the one who asks you, and do not turn away from the one who wants to borrow from you.

You have heard that it was said, 'Love your neighbor and hate your enemy.' But I tell you, love your enemies and pray for those who persecute you, that you may be children of your Father in heaven. He causes his sun to rise on the evil and the good, and sends rain on the righteous and the unrighteous. If you love those who love you, what reward will you get? Are not even the tax collectors doing that? And if you greet only your own people, what are you doing more than others? Do not even pagans do that?

Be perfect, therefore, as your heavenly Father is perfect."

—Matthew 5:38-48 (NIV)

THE SERMON

Consider the case of one of my relatives. He served in the U.S. military (a worthy profession), after which he went to Bible school, and became a pastor. After a while, he felt God calling him to the mission field, and answered that call. He spent some time in a foreign country as a missionary.

All of these are commendable occupations. Service to our great country, then going on to serve the people of God. Those are things to be proud of, right? I think so.

Now hold that thought; we'll get back to him in a few minutes.

The timeline of the "ideal life" could be as follows. Grow up, survive high school, go to college, get a job, get married, have kids, work your job until you are 65, retire with a healthy pension, and enjoy the rest of your life surrounded by friends, children, and grandchildren. In a nutshell, that is what is being sold to us as the "American Dream." But what if there is more to life than 30 years on the job, and a gold watch to show for it? What if there is another standard by which we can judge success, other than what the world has defined as "accomplishment"?

Life can be lived on a higher plane by those of us who know Christ. We are called by Him to go beyond what is normal and expected—to go beyond the requirements of society, with its rules and expectations. This drive—this injunction—to meet the "grading curve" of this world with a standard so far above its own is not a corporate or nationalized thought process. Instead, it comes from a Source whose ways are higher than our ways, and whose thoughts are higher than our thoughts.

BE WILLING TO GO FURTHER

"If anyone slaps you on the right cheek, turn to them the other cheek also. And if anyone wants to sue you and take your shirt, hand over your coat as well."

Let me make something clear from the start. This passage is not a reference to civil government. If a foreign country attacked the United States and blew up Los Angeles, we would not say, "Here you go, take Chicago too." By no means! We would respond in much the same way we responded after December 7, 1941, or September 11, 2001. If society does not judge criminal behavior with fitting punishment, the result is quite simple: chaos. Judges who are charged with upholding the laws of the land cannot, and must not, turn the community's "other cheek." In ancient justice, the command "an eye for an eye" was a good one. The laws were enforced by magistrates, and it made sure that the judgment fit the crime; not too lenient, but not overly stringent.

This is a foreboding of vigilante justice. A vigilante is a self-appointed doer of justice. It is when a person takes it upon himself to be the judge, jury, and executioner in the face of a certain crime. Besides being against the commands of God regarding justice, vigilante justice can lead to vendetta. *Vendetta* is a "blood feud." The mafia was notorious for practicing vendetta. In a famous line from the movie *The Untouchables*, officer Jimmy Malone sums up the spirit of vendetta: "He pulls a knife, you pull a gun. He sends one of yours to the hospital, you send one of his to the morgue!"[35]

Vendetta, when carried to its logical conclusion, leaves no one standing. It is a vicious cycle in which bloodshed leads to more bloodshed (leading to yet more bloodshed). This line of thinking flies in the face of the grace which Jesus taught us in this passage. As blood-bought individuals, we are not to exact revenge. Paul recognized this

THE SERMON

when he said, *"Do not take revenge, my dear friends, but leave room for God's wrath, for it is written: 'It is mine to avenge; I will repay,' says the Lord"* (Romans 12:19 NIV).

In using the words "cheek" and "coat," Jesus is talking about an insult on a personal level. Throughout history and in certain cultures, for someone to slap another's cheek was considered an insult, or even a challenge. Stealing someone's cloak could be considered an act of provocation. In this verse in Matthew, Jesus is telling us not to allow ourselves to be lured into a fight. By not reacting negatively to such an affront, you are taking the ammunition from the weapon of the enemy.

In our social-media age, it is easy to react to things we see, whether fake news, others' opinions, or someone just trying to pick a fight online. During election years, I've seen online arguments reach a fevered pitch. I have one person in particular whom I love dearly, but we don't see eye-to-eye politically. During political seasons, this person is not sparing in their opinions of some of the candidates I support. Often, this person tries to bait me into arguments with incendiary remarks in emails and messages. However, as anyone will attest to, it takes (at least) two to argue. So, what do I do when I get one of these messages? I have a choice. I can either be reactive, push back, and start an argument that, although I may be right, nobody ever really wins (and risks damaging the relationship). Or, I can make the decision ahead of time that I am not going to talk politics with this person, be proactive in love, and diffuse the situation before it ever starts. I choose the latter.

There was once a well-known pastor who served as the associate pastor at a large First Baptist church. Shortly after arriving (and before he was well-known), the senior pastor left, and the associate pastor (we'll call him Pastor Bill) began to perform the preaching duties. While the pulpit committee went in search of a new pastor, the church entered into a season of prosperity, and it soon became obvious that the congregation wanted Pastor Bill to become the new senior pastor.

Once this became obvious, a few deacons, as well as members of the pulpit committee, got together and asked Pastor Bill to leave. Instead of leaving, Pastor Bill called for a vote in the church. This enraged this small group, as they knew they had no chance of winning if it came to a vote. One Sunday, a deacon charged the pulpit during a service to read a prepared statement. He physically pushed Pastor Bill out of the way and angrily began reading his statement. The more he read, the angrier he became, until he finally turned to Pastor Bill and slapped him in the face.

Pastor Bill did nothing, except to turn the other cheek. His lack of negative reaction ended the battle.

The word *cheek* used in this passage refers to your person. The word *coat* is a reference to your possessions. It is important that you always place your emphasis on relationships over possessions. The only things you will take to Heaven are the people you have introduced to Christ. Your battle cry should always be, "Souls before stuff."

The phrase in this passage about going the second mile has to do with purpose. Purpose is represented by time and labor. With today's busy lifestyles, time is a very important commodity, and there is a natural inclination to want to see a reward from the work we do. Yet, as Christians, we must endure some hurts and hardships and put up with injustice if we ever want to be a saving force in our society. The Christian life is about living the life of a witness—a living example of what the love of Jesus and the grace of God are about. In the areas of personal relationships, we must not even allow revenge to be in our vocabulary. Our first response to unfairness or injustice should always

THE SERMON

be to "go the second mile." In ancient Rome, a Roman soldier could legally compel a Jew to carry his pack one mile. The second mile would be done to be a witness.

I was once travelling home from a visit to seminary with a fellow pastor, a man named Richard. We ran out of gasoline, and were forced to walk to the nearest gas station, which was about a half-mile up the street. The owner of the station got a gas can, filled it up, and gave us a ride back to our car. We put the gas into the tank, then drove the car back to his station and filled it up the rest of the way. Richard then asked the owner how much we owed him for the half-mile trip. The owner, sensing the potential of a bona fide "gotcha" moment, gave us a big, sly, toothless grin and said, "That'll be fifteen dollars."

Fifteen dollars? You have got to be kidding! This was 1969, when the average price of a gallon of gas was 35 cents. Fifteen dollars was highway robbery!

Well, regardless of what I may have been thinking at the time, I'll never forget what Richard did. He never flinched. He never winced. He simply reached into his pocket and pulled out a twenty, handed it to the man, smiled, and said, "God bless you."

Suddenly, the owner's demeanor changed. The "I'm so clever" grin melted from the man's face, and he began to shake uncontrollably. Richard then looked him squarely in the eyes and said, "Sir, have you ever been saved?" Like the thief who hung on the cross next to Jesus and saw—through a ravaged, beaten body—a Savior who was his only hope, this "highway robber" accepted the love of Jesus because of a man who thought the soul of a thief was worth more than fifteen dollars.

The act of giving is the faith response to the actions of others.

LOVE MORE DEEPLY

"You have heard that it was said, 'Love your neighbor and hate your enemy.' But I tell you, love your enemies and pray for those who persecute you, that you may be children of your Father in heaven. He causes his sun to rise on the evil and the good, and sends rain on the righteous and the unrighteous. If you love those who love you, what reward will you get? Are not even the tax collectors doing that? And if you greet only your own people, what are you doing more than others? Do not even pagans do that?" (Matthew 5:43-47 NIV).

It was a quiet evening in the spring of 1981 when Michael Donald went to the store for his sister. Michael was a 19-year-old African-American man living in Mobile, Alabama. On that same evening, Josephus Anderson was being tried in court for the murder of a police officer in Mobile. Anderson, also an African-American, had killed a white police officer. The trial culminated that evening with the news of a "hung jury," prompting the judge to declare a mistrial. This verdict infuriated members of the UKA—the United Klans of America (a chapter of the notorious Ku Klux Klan). Upon hearing the verdict, two members of the UKA drove around Mobile, looking for a random African-American to take revenge against.

Unlike Anderson, Michael Donald's only crime was being in the wrong place at the wrong time. UKA members Henry Hays and James Knowles spotted Michael, and forced him into their car. They then drove him to a secluded place, beat and strangled him, slit his throat, and hung his mutilated body from a tree.[36]

Subsequently, both Knowles and Hays were convicted of the crime, with Knowles being sentenced to life in prison, and Hays being sentenced to death. But the legal action didn't end there. In an attempt to uncover the depth of the conspiracy, lawyers for Beulah Mae Donald, Michael's mother, filed a civil suit against the UKA. As the trial progressed, it revealed the depth of hatred that the UKA espoused. As the trial reached its conclusion, and no defense witnesses were called, James Knowles asked to address the jury. In a surprise appeal, Knowles asked the jury to hand down a guilty verdict against the UKA. He then turned to Mrs. Donald and asked for her forgiveness for his part in this horrible crime.

With a reply that shone as a stark contrast to the act of hatred that separated a beloved son from his family, Beulah Mae Donald looked into eyes of the person who had murdered her boy and said, "Son, I forgave you a long time ago."[37]

What kind of love enables a mother to forgive her son's murderer? What kind of love enables a community to embrace the family of a murderer (remember the Amish school shooting)? What kind of love allows an old man to hold the hand of his would-be assassin (Pope John Paul II)?

What kind of love stops a holy God from striking down the very people—His own creation—who mocked, beat, scourged, and murdered His only Son?

- The deeper love, as described in this passage in Matthew 5.
- The deeper love, that serves without surrendering.
- The deeper love, that blesses without cursing.
- The deeper love, that prays without retaliation.
- The deeper love, that greets without ignoring.
- The deeper love, that lives a life of uncommon grace and mercy.

- The deeper love, that goes beyond what is expected and travels beyond the average to the exceptional.

- A deeper love, that can take an offender into its arms instead of keeping him at arm's length.

LIVE MORE FULLY.

"Be perfect, therefore, as your heavenly Father is perfect."

In Matthew 5:48, the word *perfect* comes from the Greek word *telios*, which means "complete wholeness in labor, growth, mental, and moral character." This word does not mean "sinless perfection," but "full and complete." Back in verse 45, we can be "sons of our heavenly Father"; not just another child of the angels, but one like the Father Himself.

In David Wilkerson's book *The Cross and the Switchblade*, he tells of his early efforts to win gangs of New York City to Christ. He tells of the first time he encountered a young gang leader named Nicky Cruz. Wilkerson recalled the "hardest face he had ever seen" and the first words of greeting from the street-hardened rebel: "Go to Hell, Preacher!"

As Wilkerson took a step toward the young gang leader, he told him that he loved him.

"You come near me, Preacher, I'll kill you!" came the reply.

Wilkerson could have thrown up his hands, backed away in fear and frustration, and given up then and there. No one would have blamed him. Instead, he looked Nicky in the face and said, "You could do that. You could cut me in a thousand pieces and lay them out in the street and every piece would love you."[38]

THE SERMON

Wilkerson stayed the course, went above and beyond, took the chance, and love won. Eventually Nicky Cruz got saved and became a powerful voice for the redeeming love of Jesus.

That is the secret in all of this. The agape love of God in Jesus Christ makes the difference. You love your enemies by blessing them, doing good to them, and praying for them. If we are to stand any chance of living the Uncommon Life, we must go beyond the world's standard to the "cross standard."

Now, regarding the relative I spoke of earlier: This man wore several hats during his life. Among those were soldier, preacher, and missionary. While these things all seem commendable, let me shed more light on his life.

He was born in 1920. From 1944 until 1946, he served in the Navy, surviving service in the Pacific during World War II. In 1946, he entered Bible college, and pastored five different churches between 1946 and 1974.

In 1974 (at the age of 54), he and his wife moved to Kenya, Africa. They served as missionaries in Kenya until 1983.

After returning from Africa in 1983 (at age 63), he went on to serve as pastor in seven more churches throughout New England. In 2004, his beloved wife passed away. They had been married for 63 years.

In 2008 (at the age of 88), he became the pastor of a small church in New Hampshire. At the age of 91, he was still serving his small congregation as pastor, as well as leading Bible studies in his home. When asked why he kept doing what he was doing and had not retired, he said, "I just think the Lord wants me to be busy; not sitting around doing nothing." [39]

In 2012, just months before turning 92, he succumbed to pulmonary fibrosis (which he had suffered with for some time). He lived a life of faith; a life lived for others, a life lived for a Savior he loved deeply and trusted implicitly. On that morning, when he closed his eyes to rest, and opened them in the presence of God, he finally heard the words he had lived a lifetime to hear: "Well done, good and faithful servant! Enter in!"

A life that is lived doing what is required is commendable. However, a life that performs beyond all expectations, going farther than compelled, giving more than required, loving deeper than most consider reasonable, and living more fully than most think possible . . .

- That is a life reflecting the image of the Father.
- That is a life modeling a love that went all the way to Calvary.
- That is the Uncommon Life.

THE SERMON

KEY QUESTIONS TO PONDER
Chapter 8: *Great Expectations*

1. Read Matthew 5:38-40. These verses (and others) have been used by some to teach that we should never go to war, or defend our country. Is this what the Old and New Testament teach? If not, why not? No opinions, please. Use Scripture to back up your statements.

2. Based on Jesus' teaching in Matthew 5:38-48, do you think the pastor who was punched was right in "turning the other cheek"? What was the reaction of the church when they saw how he handled the situation? What would you do?

3. Jesus said, *"Be perfect, therefore, as your heavenly Father is perfect."* Did Jesus teach that in order to love God and each other, we must live a sinless life? If not, what does the word *perfect* mean here?

Chapter 9
THE SECRET OF LIFE
Knows the Power of Sacred Secrets

"Be careful not to practice your righteousness in front of others to be seen by them. If you do, you will have no reward from your Father in heaven. So when you give to the needy, do not announce it with trumpets, as the hypocrites do in the synagogues and on the streets, to be honored by others. Truly I tell you, they have received their reward in full. But when you give to the needy, do not let your left hand know what your right hand is doing, so that your giving may be in secret. Then your Father, who sees what is done in secret, will reward you.

And when you pray, do not be like the hypocrites, for they love to pray standing in the synagogues and on the street corners to be seen by others. Truly I tell you, they have received their reward in full. But when you pray, go into your room, close the door and pray to your Father, who is unseen. Then your Father, who sees what is done in secret, will reward you. And when you pray, do not keep on babbling like pagans, for they think they will be heard because of their many words."

—Matthew 6:1-7 (NIV)

THE SERMON

Every few years, the world is held spellbound as we witness the Summer Olympic Games—the gathering of the best athletes from every nation vie for medals that will forever tell the story that they are, for at least a few moments, the best in the world. Regardless of their race, nationality, gender, or religion, the one common denominator of all of these athletes is discipline. They have travelled a long road on their arduous journey for what one song calls "One Moment in Time."

One athlete who is very familiar with every bump in the path is swimmer Michael Phelps. After capturing the gold in multiple events in both the 2004 and 2008 Olympics, Phelps was photographed in 2009 with drug paraphernalia. Being in a situation that was deemed "beneath that of an Olympian," many people afterwards questioned his commitment as an athlete going forward, and whether or not he would be a contender at the 2012 Olympics. On July 31, 2012, Phelps put all doubts to rest when he stood atop the medal platform to become the most decorated Olympian of all time. By the end of his events in the London Games, his career Olympic medal tally was 22, shattering the 18-medal record held by Ukrainian gymnast Larisa Latynina since 1964.

Kingdom citizens here on earth also compete in the contest of the ages. With precious human souls hanging in the balance, today's church cannot afford to be flabby, out of shape, short of breath, and ill-trained. There is for all of us a race to be run, battles to be fought, and crowns to be won.

Across the first 18 verses of chapter 6, three aspects of spiritual discipline are required of every Kingdom citizen. These disciplines are spelled out in verses 3-6 and 16-19.

THE DIMENSIONS OF SPIRITUAL DISCIPLINE

1. *Charitable giving* (outward flow). A popular song sung in church youth groups and around retreat campfires in the 1970s contained the line, "They'll know we are Christians by our love." While there are many ways for Christians to manifest the love of Jesus to the world around us, one way that typically attracts the attention of a cynical, secular society more than most is charitable giving. However, charitable giving for the Christian means so much more than money; it means time, material resources (other than money), and talent. It means being willing to give *all* that we are, not just what we have in our pockets or bank accounts.

2. *Prayer* (upward flow). In the busyness of our 21st-century lives, this discipline is the easiest to maintain, yet is so often neglected. For some reason, we think it is easier to fret and stress over the events in our lives, rather than bring them to our Heavenly Father in prayer. He is intimately aware of every detail of our lives, yet we so often keep Him at arm's length. He is concerned about *every* event and aspect, yet we want to compartmentalize His influence in our lives between the secular and the sacred. If we truly belong to Him, everything in our lives is sacred in His sight.

3. *Fasting* (inward flow). If prayer is the discipline that is neglected with many of us, then fasting is the lost discipline. In a culture that refuses to deny anything this world has to offer, denying self is, more often than not, out of the question. Yet, that is what Jesus commands us to do in Matthew 16:24: *"Whoever wants to be my disciple must deny themselves and take up their cross and follow me"* (NIV). Fasting is a symbolic act of our willingness to do this very thing Jesus asks of us.

THE SERMON

THE PRETENSION OF SPIRITUAL DISCIPLINE

Hypocrite comes from the Greek phrase which means "two-faced." It was the word used for the two masks, one happy and one sad, that together comprise the symbol of actors and the theatre. A hypocrite acts religiously to get the plaudits of people. You and I need to ask ourselves how much of what we do is for the applause and approval of others.

THE COMPENSATION FOR SPIRITUAL DISCIPLINE

Those who do what they do for human applause have their reward now. For most people, their spiritual labors go unseen and unnoticed in this life. However, Matthew 6:1-18 tells us of a *"Father who sees"* and *"rewards."*

In these eighteen verses, the Father is mentioned ten times. This should give us an inkling of how important these disciplines are in God's economy. They have the ability not only to transport us into His presence, but also to prepare us for our threefold battle:

1. *We battle the world.* Our giving breaks the hold of worldliness (see 1 John 2:15-17). I have heard, from time to time, Christians talk about lost material possessions and use the phrase, "Oh well, it's all gonna burn up anyway." A simple yet profound statement.

By realizing that every possession we have on this earth is temporal, and having the willingness to give up anything that He requires of us, we create an atmosphere in which the enemy cannot use the things of this world to lure us away from the battlefield into compromise and ineffectiveness.

2. *We battle the devil.* Prayer routs the enemy. Matthew 6:13 says, *"Deliver us from the evil one."* Ephesians 6:10-17 describes the

"whole armor of God" that the Christian must put on daily, in order to have any effectiveness for the Kingdom of God. However, of all of the armor listed in this passage, everything described is protective (or defensive) except the weapon listed in verse 17: *"Take the helmet of salvation and the sword of the Spirit, which is the word of God."*

Tied inextricably to that weapon is the "arm" that swings it (v. 18): *"And pray in the Spirit on all occasions with all kinds of prayers and requests. With this in mind, be alert and always keep on praying for all the Lord's people."*

Prayer is the hand that wields the weapons of praise and the Word.

3. *We battle the flesh.* Fasting overcomes the power of the flesh. Fasting says "no" to the body. Fasting allows the Spirit to say to this remnant of Adam (the flesh), "You will *not* control me!" Fasting is an outward exercise and portrayal of what it means to deny our flesh, take up our cross, and follow Jesus.

We may never know how many opportunities we have missed in advancing the Kingdom of God because of our unwillingness to exercise this discipline of fasting. We may never realize the assignments that our Holy Commander has given to other, more obedient soldiers in His army simply because we have proven ourselves to be undisciplined and undependable, as evidenced by our own inability to deny our flesh. Fasting is much more than just giving up a meal occasionally, or denying ourselves a luxury once a year; it is a discipline in which we prove our willingness and commitment to make the larger sacrifice for the cause of Christ by sacrificing the basest of human desires for a specified period. It is an outward manifestation of a heart that says, "Lord, wherever You go, I will go. Whatever You ask, I will do."

THE SERMON

In the arsenal of the Kingdom of God we've discussed, there is no weapon greater than prayer. It is the secret weapon of the believer, and knows no limits—geographical, physical, psychological, chronological, or circumstantial. Secret prayer is the main strategy in a formidable battle plan that Satan cannot stop.

William Cowper wrote, "Satan trembles when he sees the weakest Saint upon his knees."[40]

The kneeling Christian is the invincible Christian. Through the power of the Holy Spirit, we can conquer any fear, move any mountain, leap any hurdle, or overcome any obstacle, all from our primary offensive position—our knees. While some would see falling to our knees as a position of surrender, for the Christian, this is the position in which we can do the most damage offensively. By surrendering to our Commander, the Captain of the hosts of Heaven, we ourselves become a weapon in front of which the strongholds of the enemy cannot stand, and His perfect will is accomplished *on earth as it is in Heaven.*

However, in order to be the empty vessel that He can use, or the "holy howitzer" with which He storms the gates of Hell, we must remember four principles regarding prayer.

1. The Principle of Sincerity—an Open Heaven

"When thou prayest . . ."

This phrase starts off with an assumption: It assumes that we will, in fact, pray. Prayer is not an option; it is a Kingdom requirement. Prayer is our lifeline to Heaven, our hotline to the throne of God. Jesus said, *"Men ought always to pray, and not to faint"* (Luke 18:1 KJV). We are commanded, *"Pray without ceasing"* (1 Thessalonians 5:17 KJV).

OK, so maybe you don't hear "When thou prayest" in your head (spoken with a particularly thick British accent), but any prayer offered must come from a sincere heart. All of the flowery words, Shakespearean prose, and King James vocabulary in the world cannot make up for a heart that offers up prayers that are insincere and empty. Heartless, thoughtless prayer makes it as high as the ceiling, and as far as the sound of the voice reciting the words. However, heartfelt and passionate prayer reveals the key found in Jeremiah 33:3 (NIV): *"Call to me and I will answer you and tell you great and unsearchable things you do not know."*

Sincere prayer is the key that unlocks simple truth:

- Implication—you will pray: participation in the act of prayer.

- Imputation—you will believe: believing in your authority to pray as a blood-bought child of God.

- Impartation—you will receive: receiving gifts, revelation, and answers from your Heavenly Father, based on your prayer of faith.

2. The Principle of Secrecy—the Shut Door

"But when you pray, go into your room, close the door and pray to your Father."

Andrew Murray said: "Let it be your business every day, in the secrecy of the inner chamber, to meet the holy God. You will be repaid for the trouble it may cost you. The reward will be sure and rich" (*The Prayer Life*). [41]

Prayer offered to the glory of people does not move Heaven, bind Satan, nor release the sinner. The glorious truth is that the Father is found in the secret place. The Heavenly Father has a secret meeting place for every believer who will keep that divine appointment.

THE SERMON

Secrecy is vital to our praying. Secret prayer that goes unobserved and unnoticed avoids ostentation and the temptation to pray to the "listening ears" of others. When we approach prayer in undisturbed secrecy, it creates for us an atmosphere that allows us to totally focus on the Father and His word. It is in that solitude that we can operate in great freedom of expression.

Hymn writer Austin Miles expressed the need for secrecy in these words:

> *I come to the garden alone*
> *While the dew is still on the roses.*
> *And the voice I hear,*
> *Falling on my ear,*
> *The Son of God discloses.*
> *And He walks with me,*
> *And He talks with me,*
> *And He tells me I am His own.*
> *And the joy we share*
> *As we tarry there,*
> *None other has ever known.* [42]

There are some things I can only tell my Father in Heaven. There are some things that others simply would not understand. There are some burdens that only God can share.

"He who dwells in the secret place of the Most High shall abide under the shadow of the Almighty" (Psalm 91:1).

That "secret place" is the place of prayer. It is the place where pretense is cast aside, and we lay our hearts out, exposed to the God who sees every part. Here is, indeed, the place of God's overshadowing.

THE SECRET OF LIFE

3. The Principle of Simplicity—the Expectant Heart

"And when you pray, do not keep on babbling like pagans, for they think they will be heard because of their many words. Do not be like them, for your Father knows what you need before you ask him" (Matthew 6:7-8 NIV).

The Lord Jesus warns of "vain repetitions" and "much speaking" (KJV). Prayer does not require a "holy language" that has absolutely nothing in common with reality. There are no "minimum length" requirements on prayer. It is the depth of the heart that matters to God— not the depth of our verbiage or the marathon length of our supplication.

A clear illustration of this truth is seen in 1 Kings 18, when the prophets of Baal prayed long and loud without receiving an answer. The Bible says they called out to their god from morning until evening, crying out, prophesying, and cutting themselves. Yet, for all of their passionate and expressive devotion (even in the face of Elijah's ridicule), their prayers went unanswered. In contrast, Elijah's simple and forthright prayer brought down fire from Heaven, instantly.

In Luke 18:9-14, Jesus contrasts the elaborate and self-righteous prayer of the Pharisee with the simple, repentant prayer of a publican (tax collector).

> *To some who were confident of their own righteousness and looked down on everyone else, Jesus told this parable: "Two men went up to the temple to pray, one a Pharisee and the other a tax collector. The Pharisee stood by himself and prayed: 'God, I thank you that I am not like other people—robbers, evildoers, adulterers—or even like this tax collector. I fast twice a week and give a tenth of all I get.'*

THE SERMON

> *"But the tax collector stood at a distance. He would not even look up to heaven, but beat his breast and said, 'God, have mercy on me, a sinner.' I tell you that this man, rather than the other, went home justified before God. For all those who exalt themselves will be humbled, and those who humble themselves will be exalted'"* (NIV).

Jesus makes it clear that the publican and his seven-word prayer touched the heart of God. This despised and deplorable tax collector walked away in a righteousness not of his own making, justified through God.

I once heard about a little girl who was being chased by a dog. After she made it to safety, her mother asked her how she had escaped. She said, "I said my A.B.C.'s and said, 'Please God, make a prayer out of them!'" God saw her heart and rescued her.

4. The Principle of Sovereignty—the Loving Father

"Blessed are the pure in heart, for they will see God" (Matthew 5:8 NIV).

Our prayers can be offered in perfect trust and serenity, for God knows our needs. We may not always ask in the right way, or ask for the right thing, but it's OK. God in His sovereignty sorts it out.

Recording artist Michael McDonald wrote a song called "East of Eden," in which he asks, "Does He see us here? Are we precious in His sight?"

For a lot of people, that might seem almost sacrilegious. One might say, "God is a God of love, and it is disrespectful to ask such a question, or to have such a view of Him." However, the Bible is filled with examples of people questioning God. Sarah, Gideon, Job,

THE SECRET OF LIFE

various psalmists, and even Jesus himself are some of the people in the Bible who questioned God.

God never struck them dead for asking an honest question. He never railed against a query born out of desperation, hurt, fear, or anguish. Although we often fail to remember (or even understand) what the sovereignty of God means, He never forgets what our humanity means. When we call out to God in prayer, He *always* answers.

Sometimes, God says NO. He sees what we cannot see, and withholds something from us for our good.

Sometimes, God says SLOW. Our timing may not be in agreement with His, so we must wait.

Sometimes, God says GO. He gives us immediately that for which we have prayed.

Yet, regardless of the answer, in the end, the act of prayer comes back to faith. Do you have the faith to believe God knows what He is doing, even when you don't have a clue? Do you trust Him enough that, even if you don't receive the answer you wanted, you still believe He is in control? Do you believe in the sovereignty of God?

God has so ordered the universe that He does nothing but in answer to prayer. He implores us to pray. It is His divine plan at work in our world. God does not need our prayers, but we need to pray. God does require our prayers, not to overcome His reluctance, but to lay hold of His willingness. Prayer is God's proving ground for believers.

Prayer rests upon the sovereignty of God who both planned for and expects whatever may come. He already knows our needs. The question is, "Do we know our real needs?" Prayer recognizes the need for God, and rebukes self-sufficiency and pride.

THE SERMON

Sometimes praying is tough (at least it has been for me). But if we can hang on, even by the thinnest thread, to the presence of God, and the truth that He is good and has our best interests at heart, He will give us what we need to make it through this life. If we can get to that point, even if we still don't "get it," He gives us the grace to still be standing at the finish line. There, we will fully understand the words of Paul in Ephesians 6:13, "And having done all, to stand."

Since prayer is a divine key to the Kingdom, and it is God's special secret weapon, I leave you with three questions to ponder:

1. Are you praying according to these principles?

2. Do you have a secret devotional life?

3. Have you learned to talk with the Lord?

   Alone with Jesus, my dearest friend,
   What joy to spend an hour with Him.
   He bids me come and share awhile,
   Basking in the sunshine of His smile.

   —Author unknown

THE SECRET OF LIFE

KEY QUESTIONS TO PONDER
Chapter 9: *The Secret of Life*

1. Read Matthew 6:1-18. Jesus points out three aspects of spiritual discipline that are required of every Kingdom citizen. These disciplines are spelled out in verses 3-4, 5-6, and 16-19.

Name them. Discuss the importance of each:

1. _____ _____. (outward flow)

2. _____. (upward flow)

3. _____. (inward flow)

2. Spiritual discipline prepares us for spiritual battle. Name the three areas that concern Christians the most. Read 1 John 2:15-17; Ephesians 6:10-20.

1. The W _____

2. The F _____

3. The D _____

3. If prayer is the strongest weapon of the Church, why don't Christians pray more?

Chapter 10
THE NUTRITIONAL VALUE OF SOUL FOOD
The Life that Knows How to Pray

"This, then, is how you should pray:

*'Our Father in heaven, Hallowed be Your name,
Your kingdom come, Your will be done,
on Earth as it is in heaven.
Give us today our daily bread.
And forgive us our debts, as we also have
forgiven our debtors.
And lead us not into temptation, but deliver
us from the evil one.'*

*For if you forgive other people when they sin against
you, your heavenly Father will also forgive you. But if
you do not forgive others their sins, your Father will
not forgive your sins."*

— Matthew 6:9-15 (NIV)

Mahalia Jackson was considered the "queen" of gospel music. As one of the most influential gospel singers of all time, Jackson recorded around 30 records, and sold millions of copies. She once had this to say about prayer: "Faith and prayer are the vitamins of the soul; man cannot live in health without them." [44]

THE SERMON

Although she died in 1972, Jackson's influence can still be heard today, not only by listening to her timeless recordings, but also by other artists she discovered, mentored, and poured her life into.

As Christians, we have a mentor who is all-wise, all-knowing, and eternal. His Kingdom is without end, and His Word lives through the ages. During His life on earth, His classes were held on boat decks, upper rooms, and mountainsides. Today, any time we open His Word to seek after more of Him, His Holy Spirit is there to instruct us in His ways. So, today, we shall attend the "University of Prayer." Class is now in session.

From Jesus' Sermon on the Mount, we find His clearest teaching and instruction on prayer. Here are a couple of great quotes that I have heard regarding prayer:

- "More things are wrought by prayer than the world dreams of."

- "The church advances upon her knees."

Prayer is our spiritual breath of life. Prayer does not "move God" or "persuade God." Prayer moves us to where God is working in our lives. Prayer tunes our spiritual antenna to Heaven's frequency.

Prayer pleases God, and it is obvious from Scripture that He expects us to pray. In Jeremiah 33:3, we have a command and a promise: *"Call to me and I will answer you and tell you great and unsearchable things you do not know"* (NIV).

In Matthew 7:7, Jesus' own words bear out this expectation: *"Ask and it will be given to you; seek and you will find; knock and the door will be opened to you"* (NIV). In this verse (and many others throughout Scripture), we find the blessings of Jehovah are numerous, and He is determined to pour them out on His people. He just requires us to ask.

Looking at the model prayer, we find *five positive principles* of prayer.

1. PRAYER AFFECTS WORSHIP.

"Our Father who art in Heaven, Hallowed be Thy name."

This prayer begins with praise to the Father and worship of His great name. You are in an atmosphere of prayer when you understand . . .

- *The change in your life.* The devil was once your father, but now you have been adopted into the family of God. With God as your Father, you are in a new family that stretches through the ages, from eternity to eternity.

- *The Church in your life.* Notice that the phrase is "our Father," not "my Father." When you were saved, you became a part of the family of God. Where you were once alone, you are alone no longer. With God as your Father, you are a joint-heir with Jesus himself, as well as with brothers and sisters from all nations and races, from the beginning of time until the end of time as we know it.

- *The character of God in your life.* The phrase "Hallowed be Thy name" recognizes the holiness of God's character. Because He is righteous and pure, He alone should reign in our lives. His many names describe His character:

  Elohim – God

  Jehovah—I Am

  Jehovah-Tsidkenu—Our Righteousness

  Jehovah-Shalom—Our Peace

THE SERMON

Jehovah-Rophe—Our Healer

Jehovah-Jireh—Our Provider

Jehovah-Nissi—Our Banner

Jehovah-Rohi—Our Shepherd

Jehovah-Sabaoth—Our Rest.

2. PRAYER AFFECTS OUR WILL.

"Thy Kingdom come, Thy will be done on earth as it is in Heaven."

Our Father rules over the Kingdom of the ages. He is the Great King, and He has a will for earth. Prayer discovers what God has decreed in Heaven, and moves that to earth. You and I are in the binding and loosing ministry on this earth (Matthew 16:18-19).

When Jesus prayed in Gethsemane, we see the conflict between the "human Jesus" and the "divine Jesus." We might think of Jesus on earth in 50/50 terms: 50 percent human, 50 percent deity. Rest assured, He was 100 percent both, and subject to the conflict that being both involved. We see this no more clearly than when Jesus voices the request, *"Father, if it is possible, may this cup be taken from Me"* (Matthew 26:39 NIV). Being God, Jesus knew the human agony and torture that He was about to go through and, in one last request, wanted to know if He could opt out. However, we see in His next breath the resolve and strength He gained through prayer. No sooner had the words left His lips that He knew the answer: *"Yet, not My will, but Yours be done."* At that point, Jesus looked into Heaven and saw with fresh perspective the purposes of the Father in redemption. Hebrews 12:1-2 records that moment in the life of Jesus when He saw with joy a redeemed humanity:

Therefore, since we are surrounded by such a great cloud of witnesses, let us throw off everything that hinders and the sin that so easily entangles. And let us run with perseverance the race marked out for us, fixing our eyes on Jesus, the pioneer and perfecter of faith. For the joy set before him he endured the cross, scorning its shame, and sat down at the right hand of the throne of God (NIV).

Prayer gives us the ability to see God's will in our circumstances. And even in the particularly tough times when that is seemingly impossible, prayer gives us peace that we can trust God for an outcome we cannot see, but know He can see.

3. PRAYER AFFECTS OUR WALK.

"Give us this day our daily bread, and forgive us our debts as we forgive our debtors."

There is an old term called "foxhole Christianity." It references the idea that, in the heat of battle, young soldiers in the foxholes of battlefields often "find religion" evidenced by impassioned and desperate prayers to God for deliverance and safety. The truth is, when life and death are the stakes, many people, regardless of religious persuasion, suddenly discover the need for prayer. However, as the verse above states, prayer should be a "daily" practice. Prayer is a regular need in our lives, and should not be relegated to Sundays and foxholes. In this passage, two areas of daily needs are addressed:

Resources. Our daily provision can be asked for. We are to pray for the right job, income, and God's provision. Prayer is not just about the "big thing." We have a Father that desires to meet the needs of our "daily grind."

THE SERMON

Relationships. We must have the proper attitude toward others, and be in a right relationship with them. If we are wrong with family, friends, and others that we work, play, and attend church with, we are not right with God. Confession of sin and failure is an important aspect of prayer. In the Catholic church, great emphasis is placed upon "confession"—the act of the parishioner confessing sins to an earthly priest. While most Protestant denominations believe in confessing our sins directly to our Great High Priest, Jesus, the act of confession is nonetheless sacred and solemn. The act of seeking forgiveness for the sincere, praying Christian should be coupled with the willingness to forgive others their "trespasses against us."

Here is the truth of God: Failure to forgive others throws a hedge around your heart that God will not penetrate; a hedge that, over time, can grow into a seemingly impregnable fortress of unforgiveness and bitterness, leaving you isolated and alone.

Amos and Andy was an early-American sitcom, playing on radio and television from the 1920s until 1960. Andy was always being slapped in the chest by an annoying friend. Finally, one day he told Amos, "I am ready for him. I have put a stick of dynamite in my coat, and when he slaps me in the chest, it will blow his hand off."[45] What Andy failed to realize was that the same dynamite that would blow the hand off his nemesis would also blow his own chest out. In seeking revenge, he would likely die himself.

Someone once said, "Unforgiveness is like drinking poison, and expecting the other person to die." We instead must make the choice to forgive. This is part of having the mind of Jesus—thinking like He thought when He prayed from the cross, "Father, forgive them."

4. PRAYER AFFECTS OUR WARFARE.

"Lead us not into temptation, but deliver us from the evil one."

There are two truths when it comes to warfare praying:

First, the defensive posture: God can protect us from walking into temptation. If we follow His leadership, we are afforded divine protection.

Second, the deliverance principle: We need to be delivered from the snags, snares, and strongholds of Satan. His power is broken through the power of prayer.

5. PRAYER AFFECTS OUR WINNING.

"For Yours is the kingdom and the power and the glory forever."

The benediction of this passage gloriously proclaims that "our Father" has resources and power at His disposal beyond measure.

He owns the Kingdom. We pray to the One who has the keys to all of the resources and riches of the universe.

He operates the Kingdom. He has the authority to do whatever needs to be done on behalf of His children. He has the authority to act on our behalf.

He is the object of the Kingdom. The goal of the Kingdom is the praise of the Father. To give Him glory, share His glory, and behold His glory is life's ultimate goal.

He offers the Kingdom. God offers citizenship to you in His forever family! Prayer is the key that unlocks the Kingdom. Trusting Christ as your personal Savior turns the lock that opens wide the doors of promise and hope as a child of Almighty God. If you have never

THE SERMON

done this, now is the time. The cornerstone of the Uncommon Life is Jesus, the *"Stone the builders rejected, who has become the Chief Cornerstone"* (see Acts 4:11).

The God we serve, love, and worship is an awesome God! As Creator of the universe, His power is on display constantly everywhere we turn. The psalmist David wrote:

When I consider Your heavens, the work of Your fingers, the moon and the stars, which You have ordained,

What is man that You are mindful of him, and the son of man that You visit him?

For You have made him a little lower than the angels, and You have crowned him with glory and honor.

You have made him to have dominion over the works of Your hands;

You have put all things under his feet, all sheep and oxen—even the beasts of the field, the birds of the air, and the fish of the sea that pass through the paths of the seas.

O Lord, our Lord, how excellent is Your name in all the earth! (Psalm 8:3-9).

This passage reflects the awesomeness of His majesty and power, yet we understand from the Lord's Prayer that He is concerned with every area of our lives, big and small.

As someone who helped Jews in Holland escape the Holocaust, Corrie ten Boom survived being incarcerated in the Ravensbrück concentration camp in World War II. She once said: "The wonderful thing about praying is that you leave a world of not being able to do something, and enter God's realm where everything is possible. He

THE NUTRITIONAL VALUE OF SOUL FOOD

specializes in the impossible. Nothing is too great for His almighty power. Nothing is too small for His love." [46]

Her words remind me of a song we have sung in church as long as I can remember. The second verse of "What a Friend We Have in Jesus" beautifully illustrates Corrie ten Boom's thoughts:

> *Have we trials and temptations?*
> *Is there trouble anywhere?*
> *We should never be discouraged;*
> *Take it to the Lord in prayer.*
> *Can we find a friend so faithful*
> *Who will all our sorrows share?*
> *Jesus knows our every weakness;*
> *Take it to the Lord in prayer.* [47]

Class, dismissed.

THE SERMON

KEY QUESTIONS TO PONDER
Chapter 10: *The Nutritional Value of Soul Food*

1. Read Matthew 6:8 and Jeremiah 33:3, and discuss the following: Why spend time praying if God already knows our needs?

2. Read Matthew 6:11-12, and then reflect on this quote: "Our daily provision can be asked for. We are to pray for the right job, income, and God's provision. Prayer is not just about the 'big thing.' We have a Father that desires to meet the needs of our daily grind."

- Do you agree or disagree with that statement?

- Do you think God really cares about where we work, or our income? Discuss.

3. Look up a definition for the word *hallowed.* Why did Jesus use that term in referring to His Heavenly Father?

Chapter 11
LIFE IN THE "FAST" LANE
Willing to Do Without for Others

"When you fast, do not look somber as the hypocrites do, for they disfigure their faces to show others they are fasting. Truly I tell you, they have received their reward in full. But when you fast, put oil on your head and wash your face, so that it will not be obvious to others that you are fasting, but only to your Father, who is unseen; and your Father, who sees what is done in secret, will reward you."

—Matthew 6:16-18 (NIV)

"What are you praying about, Fatso?"

That is not what one typically expects to hear when sitting in a counseling session.

I was one of a few pastors in a counseling/spiritual warfare session for a young woman. I had decided to quietly bow my head during the session and just pray while one of the others spoke to the woman we were trying to help. As I sat there praying, all of a sudden, I heard a strange voice speak to me.

"What are you praying about, Fatso?"

THE SERMON

I looked up to see who had spoken to me. To my surprise, it was not the woman we had been asked to come and help. It was one of the other pastors. A demon had manifested itself through one of the pastors sitting in the room. The face I recognized, but the voice was one I was unfamiliar with. We had come to deal with the spiritual warfare issues of one person, but suddenly found ourselves fighting a spiritual war on two different fronts.

So, what gives us the ability to break the power of sin? What gives us the strength to help those being crushed by the weight of the world? What allows us to see a diversion of the enemy as merely a desperate tactic of a defeated foe?

THE DISCIPLINE OF FASTING

Of all of the disciplines of the Christian life, fasting is the one that most of us avoid like the plague. Fasting is the act of giving up something, usually food, in order to focus our attention on Kingdom priorities. Our English word for the first meal of the day, *breakfast*, is simply descriptive: "break the fast." Every night when we sleep, we are, in essence, fasting. But in a culture of sit-down restaurants on every corner, fast-food "joints" everywhere in between, and entire television networks devoted to nothing but food, fasting has become the "lost discipline."

However, it is clear that the Uncommon Life is to include the discipline of fasting. The very first three words Matthew 6:16 are *"When you fast."*

Not "if," but "when." *If* would indicate that fasting is an option for the Christian. *When* indicates there is an expectation; that it is something important, imperative, and non-negotiable. God expects us to set aside time in our lives and devote it, distraction-free, to Him. However,

144

while fasting is to be an integral part of our lives, it is not meant to be broadcast to those around us. In verse 17, we are commanded to carry out our fast incognito: we are to look alert and composed, not haggard and worn out. We should "not appear to be fasting."

Fasting surrenders something physical for something spiritual. Fasting gives up the accessible for the inaccessible. Fasting gives up the fleeting recognition and admiration of those around us for a lasting reward from our heavenly Father and the applause of Heaven.

There are many types of fasts in the Scriptures, but more often than not, fasting was the giving up of food for an extended period of time. If we want to truly understand Jesus' perspective on fasting, we must turn our focus to the Old Testament. In Isaiah 58, we find detailed instruction on fasting:

> *"Is this not the fast that I have chosen: To loose the bonds of wickedness, to undo the heavy burdens, to let the oppressed go free, and that you break every yoke? Is it not to share your bread with the hungry, and that you bring to your house the poor who are cast out; when you see the naked, that you cover him, and not hide yourself from your own flesh?*
>
> *Then your light shall break forth like the morning, your healing shall spring forth speedily, and your righteousness shall go before you; the glory of the Lord shall be your rear guard. Then you shall call, and the Lord will answer; You shall cry, and He will say, 'Here I am.'*
>
> *If you take away the yoke from your midst, the pointing of the finger, and speaking wickedness, if you extend your soul to the hungry and satisfy the afflicted soul, then your light shall dawn in the darkness, and your darkness shall be as the noonday.*

THE SERMON

The Lord will guide you continually, and satisfy your soul in drought, and strengthen your bones; you shall be like a watered garden, and like a spring of water, whose waters do not fail. Those from among you shall build the old waste places; you shall raise up the foundations of many generations; and you shall be called the Repairer of the Breach, the Restorer of Streets to Dwell In.

If you turn away your foot from the Sabbath, from doing your pleasure on My holy day, and call the Sabbath a delight, the holy day of the Lord honorable, and shall honor Him, not doing your own ways, nor finding your own pleasure, nor speaking your own words, then you shall delight yourself in the Lord; and I will cause you to ride on the high hills of the earth, nd feed you with the heritage of Jacob your father. The mouth of the Lord has spoken" (vv. 6-14).

Fasting Breaks the Power of Sin.

"To loose the bonds of wickedness." Science has shown that when someone is deprived in one sensory area, it tends to sharpen their other senses. Many times, when a person is blind, they develop heightened senses of hearing and touch. When a person is hungry, and committed to fasting and prayer, they have a heightened sensitivity to the will of God, the presence of sin, and the needs of others.

Fasting Assists Those Being Crushed by Burdens.

"Undo heavy burdens." When we flee to Christ from the attraction and temptations of the flesh, He promises to exchange the heavy burden we are carrying for His yoke of instruction, which holds the promise of a gentle touch and a place of rest.

"Come to me, all you who are weary and burdened, and I will give you rest. Take my yoke upon you and learn from me, for I am gentle and humble in heart, and you will find rest for your souls. For my yoke is easy and my burden is light" (Matthew 11:28-30 NIV).

Fasting Thwarts the Works of Satan.

"To let the oppressed go free." God uses fasting to tear down demonic oppression. Jesus told His disciples that there are some demons who "can come out by nothing but prayer and fasting" (see Mark 9:29). Fasting sharpens our focus on the Word and spiritual things, thus enabling us to break all demonic oppression.

Fasting Creates Concern and Gives Aid to the Needy.

"Share your bread with the hungry, . . . bring to your house the poor, . . . when you see the naked, cover him."

"So how can my fasting help someone else?" you may ask. Isaiah 58:7 inspires us to be creative in our fasting, as a way to reach out to the poor, hungry, and in need. There are different ways we can use our resources during a fast as a way of reaching out to others:

- Take the money you would spend on food and give it to someone in need.
- Instead of allowing your food to "go bad" during your fast, invite someone less fortunate into your home and fix them a nice meal.
- Go on a shopping fast; take someone in need shopping instead.
- If you are a weekly shopper, go on your usual shopping trip, but donate your purchase to a food bank.
- Do random acts of kindness. Look for opportunities to reach out

THE SERMON

to another person with the money you save by fasting (for example, fill up a young mother's or an elderly person's gas tank).

Fasting Gives Us a Fresh Beginning with God.

"Then your light shall break forth like the morning." Sometimes, we all need to hit the "reset" button in life. While it is not necessarily a cure-all, fasting does a lot for a person by releasing a fresh perspective and renewed hope. It gives us a new energy and focus in our relationship with God. It acts as the proverbial "dawning of a new day" by helping to clear out the clutter in our minds, and refocuses our thoughts and attention on the "Giver of all good things."

Fasting Helps to Facilitate Healing.

"Your healing shall spring forth speedily." Have you noticed that sickness often leads to a loss of appetite? Fasting can bring health and healing for the one practicing that discipline. It can give you power and discernment in praying for others.

Fasting Helps Us Experience God's Presence and Protection.

"The glory of the Lord shall be your rear guard." The *kabod* of God can be defined as "the weight of His presence." While we do not see His physical presence, when God shows up, it is obvious for the person who is in tune to His Spirit. When we fight on the battlefield of life, we have the "whole armor of God" (outlined in Ephesians 6) that protects us from the attacks of the enemy. The weakest points in any armor are in the back. Because of the closeness with God that we experience when we fast, His glory (*kabod*) becomes our rear protection. Simply put: When you fast, God has your back!

Fasting Brings Certain Answer to Prayer.

"Then you shall call, and the Lord will answer; you shall cry, and He will say, 'Here I am.'"

In Exodus 20, God is giving Moses the Ten Commandments, and while discussing the second commandment "no graven image," He gives us insight into His character: *"For I, the Lord your God, am a jealous God" (v. 5).*

When we put aside the things that distract us—the things that become "graven images" in our lives—we open up the channels of communication that get clogged up. Whether it is food, television, music, technology, sports, or any other thing that takes away from the time we spend with God, He is jealous for our love, attention, and time. But in this passage from Isaiah, we find the promise that, when we fast and clear our lives from those things that we set up as idols and take our focus away from our relationship with God, He will hear us and answer. He will show up (His presence) when we give up (our distractions).

Fasting Opens the Channels for Clear Guidance and Provision from God.

"The Lord will guide you continually, and satisfy your soul in drought, and strengthen your bones; you shall be like a watered garden, and like a spring of water, whose waters do not fail." Waters that do not fail! Isaiah 58:11 is a promise for a new level of revelation and spiritual provision. Here is a promise for living water given to us without limitation. Not only will we receive the blessing ("You shall be like a watered garden"), but by comparing us to a spring of water, this denotes we will be a resource of blessing to others, continually pouring out what we receive from the Source.

THE SERMON

Fasting Releases Revival and Restoration to the Nation.

"Those from among you shall build the old waste places; You shall raise up the foundations of many generations; and you shall be called the Repairer of the Breach, the Restorer of Streets to Dwell In."

The world is in trouble, and is becoming more dangerous every day. We see terror attacks, school shootings, cybercrimes, and the fall of business and entertainment dynasties and power-brokers. We are a country in need of repair, restoration, and a return to our God-inspired foundation. But we must also remember that as Christians, our kingdom is not of this world. We are citizens of a Kingdom "whose builder and maker is God" (Hebrews 11:10), and when we make that Kingdom our focus, and discover the victory released through fasting, we can have restoration and revival in our earthly dwelling place.

As those who long to live the Uncommon Life, it is up to us to reignite the fires of restoration and revival, and begin now to raise up the foundations of many generations—generations that are to come when we have long since passed from this life. We must begin now to repair the damage done, not just by the enemy, but by our own apathy and indifference. We must heed the words of Jeremiah 6:16, where God tells Israel, *"Stand at the crossroads and look; ask for the ancient paths, ask where the good way is, and walk in it, and you will find rest for your souls."*

If we want to see the rebuilding and establishment of a strong foundation in our day, and hope for generations to come, we must return to the lost disciplines that God set forth for those who desire to follow Him to the secret place—holiness, righteousness, worship, prayer, and fasting.

KEY QUESTIONS TO PONDER
Chapter 11: *Life in the "Fast" Lane*

1. Jesus said, *"When you fast,"* not *"if"* you fast. Is He saying that fasting is not optional? What are we to take away from that statement?

2. Read Isaiah 58:6-14. The prophet gives at least ten benefits of fasting. List them.

3. Have you ever fasted? If so, why?

    To get closer to God?

    To purify your body?

    To ask God for an answer to a crisis?

    Or, for another reason?

Chapter 12
TREASURE ISLAND
Winning the Battle Against Stuff

"Do not lay up for yourselves treasures on earth, where moth and rust destroy and where thieves break in and steal; but lay up for yourselves treasures in heaven, where neither moth nor rust destroys and where thieves do not break in and steal. For where your treasure is, there your heart will be also."

—Matthew 6:19-21

It is a subject that has captivated our culture for decades (in some cases, centuries)—pirates. The tales of swashbuckling rogues with conquered ships, captured riches, and uncharted adventure have long been the subject of folklore, literature, and movies. Classic books like *Treasure Island* by Robert Louis Stevenson and *The Pirate* by Sir Walter Scott, as well as movies like the *Pirates of the Caribbean* have chronicled the escapades of famous (albeit some fictitious) pirates such as Blackbeard, Long John Silver, and Captain Jack Sparrow. Whether remembered for their actual brutality chronicled in history books, or romanticized as chivalrous bandits of the high-seas, almost all pirate stories have something in common: buried treasure.

Whether chivalrous, scandalous, brutal, or the "perfect gentlemen," most pirates had one thing in common; they were materialistic. At the

THE SERMON

end of the day, piracy was often about the loot, and the images of these scoundrels wallowing in their ill-gotten gains often accompanies the stories and legends.

So, fast-forward a couple of centuries to 2008. The U.S. economy was in full meltdown mode, with the root cause being *greed*. Whether at the upper echelons of the corporate ladder, or the worker-bees in the lower levels of the American work force, people from every walk of life were bitten by the materialism bug. Deals were made in formerly smoke-filled rooms in the corridors of power, making it easier for people to get things they could not afford, had no way of paying for, and really didn't need. How much money is enough? How many houses does one family need to own? How many cars does someone need?

Now, don't misunderstand me. I am not saying it is wrong to own nice things. I am not saying it is a sin to purchase anything other than the cheapest items you can find. However, we have become a nation that has confused wants with needs, and rights with privileges. God certainly wants to bless us all so our needs are met (which He promised; see Philippians 4:19), in order to build His Kingdom.

John Wesley said it well: "When a man becomes a Christian, he becomes industrious, trustworthy, and prosperous. Now, if that man, when he gets all he can and saves all he can, does not give all he can, I have more hope for Judas Iscariot than for that man!"[48]

I believe God wants to bless us all so that our needs will be met, and His Kingdom will be built. Jesus addresses that subject in this, the greatest of all sermons. In these verses in Matthew 5, we get the investment advice of Jesus.

The term *treasure* found in this passage is both a noun and a verb. Literally, verse 19 says, *"Don't treasure up treasures."* The word *treasure* can be defined as "what is deposited or stored up that is valuable." God has literally deposited His treasure within us. Second Corinthians 4:7 says, *"But we have this treasure in earthen vessels, that the excellence of the power may be of God and not of us."*

As human beings, we are all born with some degree of God-given potential, and that potential is magnified when it is surrendered in obedience to the Savior. Your time, talent, influence, knowledge, and wealth are considered treasures, and these treasures are meant to be invested. Paul's call to us in this verse is that we not waste His treasure.

We can invest our lives in things eternal or in things temporal, but rest assured, we are all investing in something. Investing our lives in the wrong things is the same as throwing our money away on frivolous possessions and pursuits. Investing in those things of heavenly value is a sound investment that will reap eternal dividends. Are you investing your life, or wasting it?

THE IMPERATIVE TO INVEST YOUR LIFE

In the movie *Mr. Holland's Opus*, Glenn Holland is an aspiring musician and composer. Having spent years playing for "clubs, weddings, and Bar Mitzvahs," Mr. Holland takes on a teaching job looking for a steady paycheck. Intended to just be a job he does until he gets his "big break" via the symphony he is composing, Mr. Holland begins to find the joy of investing in the lives of others. What was intended in his mind to be a short-term gig ends up being a 30-year career of investing in the lives of the young people in his community. In the end, when he is laid off due to educational budget cuts, and believes he had wasted his life, he finds out that the opposite is true. He finds that the "symphony" he has composed is in the lives of all of the students he has invested in for the past thirty years. As one former

THE SERMON

student (who happens to be the current Governor of the state) says to him: "We are your symphony, Mr. Holland. We are the melodies and the notes of your opus. And we are the music of your life." [49]

The term *"lay up"* is a present active imperative. It is a continuous command. We are commanded not to waste our lives, but to invest them in eternity.

The fact is that you are investing your life. All of us have 24 hours a day. We all have certain gifts and talents. We all have some form of wealth, whether potential or actual. We all have something we can contribute; and, we all have a choice. We can fritter away our time on this planet, or we can do something with our lives that counts for eternity.

Any time or money you donate to God's work is an investment. There are both immediate returns and eternal returns. What better way to spend your time, effort, and resources than in changing lives for now and eternity?

> *Only one life twill soon be past.*
>
> *Only what's done for Christ will last.* [50]

THE IMPORTANCE OF WHERE YOU INVEST YOUR LIFE

"Do not lay up for yourselves treasures on earth . . . but lay up for yourselves treasures in heaven."

There are two potential places for life investment. One is this earth, and the other is heaven. Where is most of your wealth invested?

In Matthew 6:19, Jesus gives us three mental pictures to describe the perils of earthly investment: moth, rust, and thieves.

In the East, a man's wealth was displayed by his clothes. Remember how Achan stole a garment in Ai that cost Israel defeat in battle? Achan confessed: *"When I saw among the spoils a beautiful Babylonian garment, two hundred shekels of silver, and a wedge of gold weighing fifty shekels, I coveted them and took them. And there they are, hidden in the earth in the midst of my tent, with the silver under it"* (Joshua 7:21).

Achan set his heart on the things that could not last, and disobeyed the expressed command of God as a result. The consequences of his actions affected not just Achan, but his entire family. His sin became a death sentence for Achan, his family, and all that he possessed. This verse is a stern and somber warning not to set our hearts on things that can wear out.

The word *rust* comes from the Greek word which means *"eating away."* It can mean the eating away of metal, or the eating away of stored resources, such as grain, by pests and disease.

The phrase *"thieves break through and steal"* comes from the Greek phrase meaning to "dig through." Houses in those days were made of clay that could be dug through for access. All of this tells us we should not invest our lives in that which can wear out, rust out, or be stolen from us.

Pastor Rick Joyner said:

> An idol is not just an inanimate object that one bows down to and worships—it is anything that we put our trust or our affections in above God. This can include our money, jobs, education, country, spouse, children, sports, pastor, favorite teacher, favorite author, or just about anything. It is no accident that famous athletes and entertainers are often called "idol," as many people's affection for them and devotion to them can easily eclipse their affection and devotion for God.[51]

THE SERMON

Sound, godly financial investment is being a good steward of the resources God has entrusted you with to carry on His work He has called you to do. However, when we become devoted to the pursuit of wealth simply for the sake of acquiring wealth, we run the risk of making that pursuit an idol. In order for any investment on this earth to be lasting, it must have a higher purpose; it must serve a purpose beyond the bank, bonds, and bills. If we want to find true joy, our lives must be invested in those things that we cannot lose—eternal things.

THE IMPLICATIONS OF HOW YOU INVEST YOUR LIFE

"For where your treasure is, there your heart will be also. The lamp of the body is the eye. If therefore your eye is good, your whole body will be full of light. But if your eye is bad, your whole body will be full of darkness. If therefore the light that is in you is darkness, how great is that darkness! No one can serve two masters; for either he will hate the one and love the other, or else he will be loyal to the one and despise the other. You cannot serve God and mammon" (Matthew 6:21-24).

So, how can you know if you are investing your life properly? The above verses indicate three tests that determine if your life is invested in the eternal.

"Where your treasure is, there will your heart be also." Heart can include "love" and "affection." What do you love? Where are your affections centered? Are they set on things in the heavenly realm, or on the things of this earth? Do you love the things of God? Do you love the Lord Jesus Christ? Do you love His people? At the end of the day, who has your loyalty?

A young couple were being comforted after their only son had died at the age of two years. While spending time with the grieving parents, the pastor noticed the boy's mother held an old teddy bear, and his father grasped a small toy soldier. The young wife cried, "Joey loved these things so much, that we love them too." As believers in Christ, our love for Him should be manifested in the fact that we love the things—people, righteousness, holiness, compassion—He loved.

At a 1975 pastor's conference in Norfolk, Virginia I heard Dr. R. G. Lee, the "prince of preachers," for the last time. Dr. Lee told the story of a young couple who were in love and planned to be married. Before the wedding could happen, World War II broke out, and Ted was compelled to enter military service, and was promptly shipped out to the war. It wasn't long before Mary received word that Ted had been wounded. His injuries were so severe that Ted wrote a letter to Mary, releasing her from her commitment and their engagement. When Mary read the letter, she said to herself and to God, *No! You will not release me, Ted!*

She got on a train and journeyed to the hospital where Ted was recovering from his wounds. When she walked into the room and saw Ted, she realized he had lost both of his arms. Ted cried out, "Oh Mary, why did you come? I can't even hug you!" Mary ran over and fell on Ted, crying, "Oh Ted, I love you, honey! I'll be your right arm and I'll be your left arm!"

They were married and lived a life of joy, serving the Lord together.

Think of our wounded Savior—the ridicule He encountered; the beating He withstood; the pain and loss of blood He endured; the nails, thorns, and spear that pierced His body. Will you confess, "Jesus, I'll be Your arms, hands, eyes, and feet upon this planet"? "I'll be faithful to You, Lord, for You have given so much for me."

When we all come to the end of our lives, we will have to face

THE SERMON

two final questions: (1) What did you gain in life that you can keep in eternity? (2) What did you give in life that will last in eternity?

Are you making any heavenly investments, or are you living for the meaningless plunder of a pirated soul, adrift on the seas of self-centeredness and selfish ambition?

The choice is yours. You can seek after earthly treasure and the fleeting prestige it brings, and rest assured that you will be buried right alongside your buried treasure, where you'll both turn to dust together.

Or you can understand your life is your treasure, and by surrendering that treasure to Jesus, the Captain of your soul, you are investing in the riches of Heaven. There, no rust or moth can corrupt or corrode, and no thief can break in and steal.

It's time to throw off your bowlines, set your sails, hoist your colors, and follow the winds of the Spirit!

KEY QUESTIONS TO PONDER
Chapter 12: *Treasure Island*

1. Read Matthew 6:19-21. Jesus said, *"Do not lay up for yourselves treasures on earth."* Are we to give away all of our "stuff" and live in poverty? Is it wrong for a Christian to have possessions? Discuss.

2. There are two potential places for life investment. One is this earth, and the other is Heaven. Where is most of your wealth invested? How are we to "lay up" treasures in Heaven? Is this literal? Or is this just a good idea?

3. Read Luke 12:15-21. Why did Jesus condemn the "rich fool"? Can you find a relationship between this parable and the Sermon on the Mount?

Chapter 13
I CAN SEE CLEARLY NOW
The Life that Has the Right Perspective

> "The lamp of the body is the eye. If therefore your eye is good, your whole body will be full of light. But if your eye is bad, your whole body will be full of darkness. If therefore the light that is in you is darkness, how great is that darkness!"
>
> —Matthew 6:22-23

The Message paraphrases Matthew 6:22-23 like this:

> "Your eyes are windows into your body. If you open your eyes wide in wonder and belief, your body fills up with light. If you live squinty-eyed in greed and distrust, your body is a dank cellar. If you pull the blinds on your windows, what a dark life you will have!"

With the death of actor Robin Williams in 2014, conversation about depression and mental health once again came to the forefront in our culture. For weeks following the apparent suicide of this beloved actor and funnyman, there was much discussion about the reality of depression, recognizing the signs of someone struggling, and ways to help a friend, loved one, or acquaintance who was suffering. However, the options for getting help for someone struggling with depression are extremely varied.

THE SERMON

Sometimes, depression is the result of a chemical imbalance in the brain, a result of heredity and genetics. In other cases, depression can be a result of life experience, the aftermath of tragedy or personal trauma. Then there is depression that comes as a result of our own poor decisions. Poor health choices, bad financial decisions, and family and relational conflict can cause depression. As someone who has dealt in the area of spiritual warfare for years, oftentimes I see depression as a byproduct of demonic activity, when a person participates in an activity, by choice or force, that opens the floodgates of demonic influence in their life, and the darkness that accompanies it.

SUFFERING IN DARKNESS

In all my years as a pastor, I cannot tell you the number of times people have described where they were at that moment as a "dark place." They make the decision to pull the "shades" on the windows of their life, not allowing the light of Jesus' love to drive the darkness away.

One such story involved a gentleman that I was counseling several years ago. He told me how he had gone through a season of depression, a depression he later believed to be demonic. He was active in his church and had a wife and children who loved him, but he could not shake the feelings of darkness that consumed his thoughts and life; darkness that was the result of poor decisions, misfortune, and setbacks in his life. At this critical time in his life and thinking, he met someone who claimed to understand what he was going through, and reached out to help him. In his attempt to escape the darkness, he clung to something that was only an illusion, and spent the next two years living in the lies of adultery, resentment, and rebellion. He told me that he knew what was right and wrong, but as his perspective had become so distorted, he just didn't care. Finally, he woke up one day and realized he had wandered far, and only wanted to get back home, but did not know how. Like so many prodigals who truly know the Father, through a miraculous series of events, the Lord dispelled the darkness in his life, brought this prodigal home, restored his family, and guided him through a period of restoration. Today, he once again serves the Lord unreservedly.

As my friend's life is evidence, how you see life determines how you live. Someone who is brought up in a loving, caring atmosphere will generally have a much different perspective than someone raised in an environment of abuse and neglect. Our own disposition or choices of rebellion versus obedience can have a remarkable impact on the lens through which we view life's events. Having the right perspective will go a long way toward releasing right actions which will, in turn, lead to a satisfying life. Today, we refer to this as a person's *worldview*.

Every person born is comprised of three characteristics: intellect, emotion, and will. In this section of the Sermon on the Mount, Jesus deals with these three characteristics. While in the previous passage (verses 19-21) we find Jesus dealing with the human heart and affections, in verses 22-23 He is dealing with the intellect, using the eye for symbolism. Whenever "eye" is singular, it refers to perspective— the view, the vision of one's life—not literal sight. It refers to one's capacity to learn and observe. "Eyes" (plural) refers to eyesight.

In our culture, there is a phrase from literature that refers to a person looking at life through "rose-colored glasses." The idea is that one's view of life is overly and/or unrealistically optimistic.

Years ago, Paulette and I toured the old ship *Queen Mary*, docked in Long Beach, California. While on the tour, we went into

THE SERMON

a stateroom where the guide pointed out that the mirrors were tinted with a rose color. He explained that the reason for the coloring was to fool passengers who were suffering from sea-sickness into thinking they did not look as bad as they felt. In this passage, Jesus teaches us the importance of viewing life undistorted.

Our perspective can be affected by any number of things: upbringing, religious belief, and personal experience are among the factors in determining our perspective. These are all elements that are a part of the experience we call "life," and everyone's perspective is constantly being shaped by the events of their lives. An old saying illustrates the truth of perspective: "I once complained that I had no shoes until I met a man with no feet."

My co-author, Dana, has lived what most would consider an Uncommon Life. Having known him now for over 25 years, I have seen the things God has done in his life with my own eyes, and I believe he can add something about having a right perspective:

> In 1983, when I was 16 years old, my dad died in a horrific car accident that almost took my life as well. I eventually made a "full" recovery, but in 2006, I began experiencing bad earaches. I went to a doctor who diagnosed me with TMJ dysfunction, a problem with my jaw. As it turned out, I had a friend who was a specialist in TMJ dysfunction, and went to visit him. A series of X-rays led to an MRI which revealed that, in the accident in 1983, my jaw had been broken, and it had gone undiagnosed for 23 years! My doctor informed me it was a miracle that I could even function normally, as my jaw was completely destroyed. The joint on one side was completely gone, and what was there was an unexplainable collection of tendons and ligaments that

had formed a makeshift joint next to where the joint should have been.

"You're a miracle, because *this* is not possible!" I was told by my doctor.

When I got this news, I was at a very low point in my life, and God used this experience to give me a fresh perspective about how much He truly loved and cared for me, and how important I was to Him. He bent the laws of physiology and medical reason to show me that His hand was on me. I was on His radar, and not forgotten or useless.

Fast forward to May 2012. I was at home alone one morning getting ready for work, when all of a sudden, I began having tightness in my chest, and a feeling of not being able to catch my breath. I tried to ignore it, thinking it would pass, but it didn't. I began to feel as though I might pass out, and decided I should probably go to the hospital, as this could possibly be a heart attack. I began to talk to God: *I refuse to believe that, after all You have brought me through, it is going to end like this. I refuse!*

As I drove myself to the hospital, I thought whatever it was would pass and I would be fine, turn around, and just go home. I continued to tell God I didn't believe He was calling it quits for me.

I got to the hospital, and after tests were run, it was discovered I had, in fact, had a heart attack. In spite of the diagnosis, my belief in God's unfinished work in my life helped me have a perspective that refused to give up. I believe God brings us through experiences in our lives not just for our benefit, but to encourage others and to glorify His name and presence in our lives. I believed

THE SERMON

> that my story wasn't over, and I still had work to do—a
> life to live, a story to tell, and people to encourage.

Since his heart attack in 2012, Dana has survived two more car accidents, a ruptured appendix, and three separate cancer diagnoses ("with more surgeries than I can remember," he said). And with each one, he continues to say the same thing: *God, I still refuse to believe that You have brought me through all of this to let it end here.* Like Dana, and everyone else who lives the Uncommon Life, we have a choice: We can either allow our circumstances to dictate our perspective, or we can trust God's hand in spite of our circumstances, and view our trials as opportunities for God to reveal Himself in a bigger way than before. As Dana, has shared with me, "I'm choosing to believe God's promise over my doctor's prognosis."

A GATEWAY TO THE SOUL

"The lamp of the body is the eye."

Living in the 21st century, we are inundated with information. Short of escaping to a secluded desert island, or escaping into an uncharted wilderness, we are hard pressed to get away from the constant barrage of data before our eyes at every turn. Television, radio, billboards, magazines, computers, and smartphones makes getting away from the flow of images, numbers, and noise nearly impossible. That is why it is so important to guard our minds regarding what we choose to see, watch, and hear. That which should govern and direct our bodies is the right vision and information flowing into our lives.

As seen in *The Message* paraphrase of our passage, it is possible for selfishness and greed to affect our perspective. Living "squinty-eyed in greed and distrust" blocks the light of the selflessness that Jesus calls us to. A life that is closed off in self-interest eventually becomes a very dark place. Tapping into *the* source of light, Jesus, requires living a life in tune with, and plugged into, His power. It is that selflessness and generosity that parts ways with a "me first" mentality and throws open the shades to the light, fullness, and power of the Uncommon Life.

In the computer world, there are viruses, malware, and spam that can corrupt and slow the operation of the computer. So it is with our minds. If our thinking is distorted by a self-interested view of life, then we will be infected by demonic viruses that will distort our actions. In I.T. circles, there is the concept *GIGO* (Garbage In, Garbage Out). If you let in just one bad stream of programming, it can crash the entire program. If you let in just one area of darkness, it can skew your perspective, and cause you to see things unclearly.

In the Bible, darkness represents sin. Just as much can be hidden in a dark place, darkness always makes sin look better than it is. In John 3:19, we read: *"And this is the condemnation, that the light has come into the world, and men loved darkness rather than light, because their deeds were evil."*

Darkness is not an element in and of itself, but is simply the absence of light. If we elevate human reason or human greed above the knowledge of God, we are in darkness, not because the darkness is greater than the light, but simply because the light is no longer present. God's presence will not reside in the presence of human pride and arrogance. God is light, and anything that we allow to dim His revelation to us can lead to disaster. If you walk into a dark room infested by cockroaches, and simply turn on the light, the roaches will scatter. When we invite the presence of God to enter the room, the roaches of greed and selfish ambition have to scatter. Light and darkness cannot co-exist, and when the light enters, the darkness must leave, and all it conceals is forced into that light.

THE SERMON

This is the message which we have heard from Him and declare to you, that God is light and in Him is no darkness at all. If we say that we have fellowship with Him, and walk in darkness, we lie and do not practice the truth. But if we walk in the light as He is in the light, we have fellowship with one another, and the blood of Jesus Christ His Son cleanses us from all sin (1 John 1:5-7).

Light allows us to see the truth about ourselves and our world. We cannot walk in darkness (actively participate in sin), and claim we have a right relationship with God. If we think we can, we are believing a lie, and are allowing ourselves to be blinded to the truth. Second Corinthians 4:3-4 puts it this way: *"But even if our gospel is veiled, it is veiled to those who are perishing, whose minds the god of this age has blinded, who do not believe, lest the light of the gospel of the glory of Christ, who is the image of God, should shine on them."*

It is Satan's desire to block the gateway (eye) of your life from the light that God desires to shine into your life. Only the life that is walking in the light can experience the intimacy of fellowship with the God of light.

So, will you choose to live wide-eyed, or squinty-eyed?

KEEPING YOUR EYE ON THE GOAL

"If therefore your eye is good, your whole body will be full of light."

This is the goal: that your life may be full of the light of God. Jesus encourages us to worship in "spirit and truth"; He was pretty adamant about it (John 4:24). Passionate worship (spirit) is a wonderful thing, and is worship that pleases God. However, worshiping "in spirit" does not mean we check our intellect at the door.

I CAN SEE CLEARLY NOW

Take music for an example. In some circles, there is the thought that, in order for a song to be worshipful, it must be ethereal and repetitive. However, I once had a musician tell me this: "I love worship music that is both worshipful and musically interesting. I love and appreciate worship music that is complex, and pushes me as a musician. We serve a creative God, and I think music that challenges my mind is a reflection of the creative power of God."

God is the author of creativity. His first recorded work is the act of Creation itself. His creative process began with the command, "Let there be light." Paul wrote, *"For it is the God who commanded light to shine out of darkness, who has shone in our hearts to give the light of the knowledge of the glory of God in the face of Jesus Christ"* (2 Corinthians 4:6).

Contrary to what the world would have you believe, it is not an "either/or" choice when it comes to faith and intellect. True faith and honest intellect (real science) can walk hand-in-hand, supporting each other as they tell the story of a God who spoke the universe into being, made every molecule and atom, and created a world of immense beauty and complexity. It is that same creative power that enters your life when you receive Jesus as your Savior. It is through Him that your potential for accomplishment is increased dramatically and exponentially. When God's self-revelation showed you Jesus Christ, and you opened your spiritual eyes, His life and His light flooded into your soul. The miracle of God that put the earth at the right angle of rotation, at the proper distance from the sun, spinning at a speed that makes day and night, in an orbit around the sun that creates wonderful seasons as well as sustains life—that same creativity is available to line things up in your life!

The words *knowledge* and *glory* in 2 Corinthians 4:6 represent

THE SERMON

perception and direction. *Knowledge* is knowing Christ as close and lovingly as a married couple. *Glory* is like the cloud that guarded and guided the children of Israel in the wilderness (Exodus 13:20-22). In the darkness of that desert experience, they had a "cloud by day" and a "pillar of fire by night."

Think about Job. His future looked dark. He had lost everything. His "friends" had crushed him with their words of self-righteous accusation and derision. However, when all was said and done, he was vindicated by God himself. The light of God's presence delivered Him from his despair and restored him. Job said, *"I have heard of You by the hearing of the ear, but now my eye sees You. Therefore I abhor myself, and repent in dust and ashes"* (Job 42:5-6).

When the light of God's presence illuminates our lives, it reveals what a wretch even the most righteous person is. The prophet Isaiah said *"all our righteousnesses are like filthy rags"* (Isaiah 64:6). Job understood this. Although considered a righteous man by earthly standards, Job recognized his unworthiness under the well-lit microscope of the holiness of God. As a result of this repentance and recognition, the Lord acted mightily on Job's behalf: *"And the Lord restored Job's losses when he prayed for his friends. Indeed the Lord gave Job twice as much as he had before"* (Job 42:10).

Don't let Satan blind you to God's goals in your life. Don't believe the lie that your current circumstances and tragedies have disqualified you from God's purpose. Don't settle for the shadows and darkness of "second best" when the light of God's presence invites you to enter in to the fullness He has waiting for you. Maybe Paul understood this when he wrote, *"The gifts and calling of God are without repentance"* (Romans 11:29). It could be that this principle was on the mind of the psalmist when he wrote: *"Incline my heart to Your testimonies, and not to covetousness. Turn away my eyes from looking at worthless things, and revive me in Your way"* (Psalm 119:36-37).

The psalmist understood our dependence on God's presence, and also our need for revival. Paul understood that, once God calls you, His calling is irrevocable; He is never going to regret the call He placed on you. Disqualification and disconnection are not in the vocabulary of the person living the Uncommon Life. In his book *All Is Grace: A Ragamuffin Memoir,* the late Brennan Manning put it this way:

> *Do you believe that the God of Jesus loves you beyond worthiness and unworthiness, beyond fidelity and infidelity—that He loves you in the morning sun and in the evening rain—that He loves you when your intellect denies it, your emotions refuse it, your whole being rejects it? Do you believe that God loves without condition or reservation and loves you this moment as you are, and not as you should be?* [52]

Well, do you?

THE EYE OF GENEROSITY

If we go back to the previous chapter, we will remember a life filled with things consumed by moths, corrupted by rust, and stolen by thieves—a life that is comprised by that which will not last. We can settle for that, or we can choose the better way, step into the light, and open our eyes to God's mission and goals for us. Jesus said, *"But if your eye is bad, your whole body will be full of darkness. If therefore the light that is in you is darkness, how great is that darkness!"* (Matthew 6:22-23).

If that which you allow into your life is darkness, then the eventual tragedy will be unspeakable. There is almost nothing more tragic

THE SERMON

than the person who thinks they are right, but are merely deceived. It is astounding how many people believe they are living a life of "enlightenment" when they are lost in the darkness of their own thought processes and selfish ambition. No ultimate good can come from a life lost in darkness and deception.

Think about the story of the wayward son in Luke 15. He thought he was going to the light of freedom. He thought that, by getting out from under his father's roof and rule, he would become enlightened by the things of the world. Yet, in the end, all he found was a deep darkness induced by selfishness and waste. What started as a quest for enlightenment ended up in the depths of loneliness, brokenness, and filth!

So, when did he come home to the light? "When he came to himself" (v. 15). The darkness that consumed him was not enough to quench the bright memories of a life with a loving and gracious father. That godly light drew him home.

"How great is that darkness." The word *great* is *poson* in Greek, meaning "immeasurable darkness." A life lived for its own self-interest and ambition is a life of darkness and loneliness. Consider this story Jesus told:

> *"There was a certain rich man who was clothed in purple and fine linen and fared sumptuously every day. But there was a certain beggar named Lazarus, full of sores, who was laid at his gate, desiring to be fed with the crumbs which fell from the rich man's table. Moreover the dogs came and licked his sores. So it was that the beggar died, and was carried by the angels to Abraham's bosom. The rich man also died and was buried. And being in torments in Hades, he lifted up*

> *his eyes and saw Abraham afar off, and Lazarus in his bosom. Then he cried and said, 'Father Abraham, have mercy on me, and send Lazarus that he may dip the tip of his finger in water and cool my tongue; for I am tormented in this flame'"* (Luke 16:19-24).

The rich man missed God. In spite of his vast wealth, when he came to the end of his life, it was his wealth that testified against him. God was sitting at the gate in the person of Lazarus, but although he had the means, the rich man did nothing to ease Lazarus's station or pain. Jesus was pretty specific about how we treat the poor. In Matthew 25:41-46, He says these words:

> *"Then He will also say to those on the left hand, 'Depart from Me, you cursed, into the everlasting fire prepared for the devil and his angels: for I was hungry and you gave Me no food; I was thirsty and you gave Me no drink; I was a stranger and you did not take Me in, naked and you did not clothe Me, sick and in prison and you did not visit Me.'*

> *"Then they also will answer Him, saying, 'Lord, when did we see You hungry or thirsty or a stranger or naked or sick or in prison, and did not minister to You?' Then He will answer them, saying, 'Assuredly, I say to you, inasmuch as you did not do it to one of the least of these, you did not do it to Me.' And these will go away into everlasting punishment, but the righteous into eternal life."*

May God help us to see what He sees! May we see others through the light of His love and acceptance. May we always be on the lookout for others in need of the light that illuminated us to grace and mercy, and share that light with those lost in darkness.

THE SERMON

So, what does it look like from your perspective? Is the light of God's presence shining right now on some area that you need to surrender to His control and purpose? Are you choking on a lie that true enlightenment can be found in some place other than at His nail-pierced feet? If you need that light to dispel the darkness, now is a good time to start. Like the prodigal, you have a Father who is looking down the road, sees you a long way off, and is waiting to run to you. He is just a prayer away.

KEY QUESTIONS TO PONDER
Chapter 13: *I Can See Clearly Now*

1. Read 1 John 1:5-7. Discuss the following statement: "Light and darkness cannot co-exist. When the light enters, the darkness must leave, and all it conceals is forced into that light."

2. Read John 3:19. What does darkness represent in the Bible?

3. What was Jesus trying to teach when He told the parable of the rich man in hell (Luke 16:19-24)?

- Did the rich man miss Heaven because of his wealth?

- Did Jesus mean Hell is a literal place?

- Did the beggar go to Heaven because he was poor?

Chapter 14
WHO'S THE BOSS?
The Life that Knows Who Is in Charge

> *"No one can serve two masters; for either he will hate the one and love the other, or else he will be loyal to the one and despise the other. You cannot serve God and mammon."*
>
> —Matthew 6:24

The Manning brothers, Peyton and Eli, won Super Bowl rings as NFL quarterbacks. In an interview with Jason Cole of Yahoo Sports in 2012, Eli said:

> *I admire Peyton and watching him on film and the throws he makes and the mechanics, I still watch in awe. He's still at that top level as far as what he has done with the football. We have a great relationship and it's a total support [system]. I call him or he calls me, like during the season last year. Especially during the playoff stretch, he would call me and just have little tidbits and pieces of advice a quarterback can talk about that you cherish.* [53]

A close, supportive family is wonderful, and there is nothing quite like having a great relationship with a sibling. But when the Mannings faced each other in a game, there was no favoritism or letting up. Each

THE SERMON

of the Manning brothers showed up with the expectation that they were going to lead their team to victory. Though, as Peyton once said, not "quite as enjoyable as it would be if you were beating somebody else," a win was still a win. The Mannings had to leave their brotherly loyalty in the locker room, choose a side, and go out on the field intent on beating their opponent.[54]

We can recall the stories told down through history of our own Civil War, when brother fought against brother, and neighbor against neighbor. The horror of having to make the decision to strike down a family member in the name of "country" is a horror most of us could never fathom. However, at some point in our lives, we all have to make tough choices—choices that can cost cherished relationships, financial gain, or peace of mind. These choices will test our loyalty to our core beliefs, our deepest convictions, and even to God himself.

Humans are made in "the image of God." Though fallen, we retain glimmers of that image. Among all living creatures given the gift of the breath of life at creation, only humankind is given a heart to love, a mind to reason and visualize, and a will to choose.

In this apex of all of Jesus' teaching, He chooses to test us in these three areas. As we previously observed:

1. What our heart loves is our treasure. Our heart will follow what we value most.

2. Our "eye" (mind, soul) is our worldview, and colors all that we do.

Now Jesus approaches the ultimate test—the human will. Our free will is a double-edged sword in that it is our greatest gift and our greatest danger. The right to freely choose our own path opens for us both the greatest opportunities and the greatest perils. The text before us asks three questions—concerning lordship, loyalty, and life.

1. THE QUESTION OF LORDSHIP

Jesus said, *"No one can serve two masters."* The word *serve* comes from the Greek *doulos*, which is the word for "bond-slave." In the Greco-Roman world, a slave could only have one master; it was both illegal and impossible to be ruled by two.

The word *master* is the Greek word *kurios*, translated to "lord" in most places in the New Testament. This refers to both Jesus Christ as well as the tithe given to Caesar. If we take this literally, and indeed make Jesus Christ our Lord, we have to understand that He will not share the throne of our lives with any other. There is an absoluteness in this statement.

In the New Testament world of Rome, the Caesar required all who lived under the scepter of Rome to confess, "Caesar is lord" annually, while offering a pinch of incense. Not to make such a confession was an offense worthy of death.

"Jesus is Lord" was the earliest confession of faith, and remains the only authentic confession of faith. If one is to be saved and become a Christ follower, then Jesus Christ must be Lord. He's the boss, forever. If He is not Lord of all, then He is not Lord at all.

If someone is not fully satisfied with their relationship with Jesus, it is probably because they have never fully surrendered all to Him. When we come to Christ, we come to Him from a position of need and peril. We are all sinners in need of a Savior, and the peril that we face is eternal separation from Him.

Imagine you are hanging from a cliff, your fingers barely grasping onto the rocky ledge. Imagine now that a hand reaches down from a secure place of safety to offer you a way of escape. In order to take

THE SERMON

advantage of the salvation at hand, you must let go of the rocky ledge, and take the hand that is offered to you. You cannot continue to hold onto the ledge if you wish to be rescued. Surrender is your only hope of escaping the peril and certain death you face.

So it is with Christ. When Jesus reaches down with His nail-pierced hand and offers us salvation, we have to let go. We must release our grip on the things of the world—the ties that bind us, and the fleeting things that offered us false security for a season. In order to be lifted to the solid Rock of safety, we must trade the death-grip we have on the things of this world, and trust His grip and His strength to save us. Only by letting go of the cliff of peril and death can we find safety and security in His arms. It is all about surrender, and the ultimate confession of all Creation, and declaration of individual surrender, is "Jesus is Lord."

> *Therefore God also has highly exalted Him and given Him the name which is above every name, that at the name of Jesus every knee should bow, of those in heaven, and of those on earth, and of those under the earth, and that every tongue should confess that Jesus Christ is Lord, to the glory of God the Father* (Philippians 2:9-11).

In His life as a servant, death on the cross, and triumphant resurrection, Jesus took His title. *"For to this end Christ died and rose and lived again, that He might be Lord of both the dead and the living"* (Romans 14:9).

2. THE QUESTION OF LOYALTY

"He will hate one and love the other, or else he will be loyal to one and despise the other."

WHO'S THE BOSS?

You cannot live your life as a spiritual schizophrenic. *Mammon* represents money, pleasure, popularity, favor, and human achievement. While there is nothing innately wrong with these things, the problems come into play when serving Christ and these desires clash. When you no longer have time for God, giving your tithes and offerings no longer matters, or the love of pleasure supersedes your desire to serve God, your loyalty can be called into question.

The truth is, this is a daily struggle for most of us. What is the best way to cope with it? Don't make wealth and position an idol.

> *Command those who are rich in this present age not to be haughty, nor to trust in uncertain riches, but in the living God, who gives us richly all things to enjoy. Let them do good, that they be rich in good works, ready to give, willing to share, storing up for themselves a good foundation for the time to come, that they may lay hold on eternal life* (1 Timothy 6:17-19).

This passage starts off with a word of caution against pride, and a warning against the uncertainty of riches. It acknowledges that pride has always been a byproduct of wealth. It reveals to us that riches were as uncertain in the first century as Wall Street is today. But it also reinforces the idea that there is great promise in using our financial resources to serve, to do good, and to further the Kingdom of God.

Learn the crucified life. Galatians 2:20 describes it: *"I have been crucified with Christ; it is no longer I who live, but Christ lives in me; and the life which I now live in the flesh I live by faith in the Son of God, who loved me and gave Himself for me."* Paul added, *"And those who are Christ's have crucified the flesh with its passions and desires"* (5:24).

THE SERMON

Our loyalty must rest with Jesus Christ alone. We must take the idols of selfish ambition, monetary gain, and earthly pleasure to the place of death at the foot of the cross of Christ. Just as Paul learned, we must also understand that we cannot be all that Christ wants us to be as long as our loyalty is divided. *"For do I now persuade men, or God? Or do I seek to please men? For if I still pleased men, I would not be a bondservant of Christ"* (Galatians 1:10).

3. THE QUESTION OF LIFE

"You cannot serve God and mammon."

The key word here is *serve*. Also, the word *love* found earlier is a key to understanding that claim; it's the word *agape*. This is the word for "absolute and unconditional devotion and service." This is not a call to quit work, nor a summons to unenjoyable living. Working hard is a Biblical concept, and there is nothing wrong with the desire to succeed, just as long as that job or that desire does not become an idol. One can also enjoy recreation, but not to the point of obsession.

When there is a legitimate choice between the Lord Jesus and anything else, He must be our top priority. Take another look at 1 Timothy 6:17: *"Command those who are rich in this present age not to be haughty, nor to trust in uncertain riches but in the living God, who gives us richly all things to enjoy."*

God give us good things to enjoy! James said, *"Every good gift and every perfect gift is from above, and comes down from the Father of lights, with whom there is no variation or shadow of turning"* (James 1:17).

The good we have in life is from God, and He must remain Lord over those things. Good things in life can become idols if our desire becomes more focused on the gift than the Giver. Paul warned Timothy: *"But those who desire to be rich fall into temptation and a snare, and into many foolish and harmful lusts which drown men in destruction and perdition. For the love of money is a root of all kinds of evil, for which some have strayed from the faith in their greediness, and pierced themselves through with many sorrows"* (1 Timothy 6:9-10).

The word *desire* means "first passion." If we become obsessed with anything or anyone more than Jesus, it is a trap of the enemy.

Ultimately, life is a series of choices. In this life, we are faced with those choices every day: Jesus or self; Jesus or money; Jesus or an idol; Jesus or a person; Jesus or an object; Jesus or entertainment; Jesus or a hobby.

So now will you choose? Before you answer that question, listen to this encounter one person had with Jesus.

> *Now behold, one came and said to Him, "Good Teacher, what good thing shall I do that I may have eternal life?" So He said to him, "Why do you call Me good? No one is good but One, that is, God. But if you want to enter into life, keep the commandments."*
>
> *He said to Him, "Which ones?"*
>
> *Jesus said, "'You shall not murder, You shall not commit adultery, You shall not steal, You shall not bear false witness, Honor your father and your mother,' and, 'You shall love your neighbor as yourself.'"*
>
> *The young man said to Him, "All these things I have kept from my youth. What do I still lack?"*
>
> *Jesus said to him, "If you want to be perfect, go, sell*

THE SERMON

what you have and give to the poor, and you will have treasure in heaven; and come, follow Me."

But when the young man heard that saying, he went away sorrowful, for he had great possessions.

Then Jesus said to His disciples, "Assuredly, I say to you that it is hard for a rich man to enter the kingdom of heaven. And again I say to you, it is easier for a camel to go through the eye of a needle than for a rich man to enter the kingdom of God."

When His disciples heard it, they were greatly astonished, saying, "Who then can be saved?"

But Jesus looked at them and said to them, "With men this is impossible, but with God all things are possible."

Then Peter answered and said to Him, "See, we have left all and followed You. Therefore what shall we have?"

So Jesus said to them, "Assuredly I say to you, that in the regeneration, when the Son of Man sits on the throne of His glory, you who have followed Me will also sit on twelve thrones, judging the twelve tribes of Israel. And everyone who has left houses or brothers or sisters or father or mother or wife or children or lands, for My name's sake, shall receive a hundredfold, and inherit eternal life. But many who are first will be last, and the last first" (Matthew 19:16-30).

This man faced a decision, and made the worst possible choice. Which will you choose?

KEY QUESTIONS TO PONDER
Chapter 14: *Who's the Boss?*

1. Read Matthew 6:24. Discuss why it is so hard for rich people to serve God.

2. Jesus said, *"No man can serve two masters."* Is it possible to be saved and still not recognize Jesus as Lord? Do you agree that "He is Lord of all, or not Lord at all"? Discuss.

3. What does "mammon" represent. Is it just money? Look up the definition and discuss its ramifications in light of today's culture of greed.

Chapter 15
MISSION IMPOSSIBLE?
The Life that Refuses to Worry

"Therefore I say to you, do not worry about your life, what you will eat or what you will drink; nor about your body, what you will put on. Is not life more than food and the body more than clothing? Look at the birds of the air, for they neither sow nor reap nor gather into barns; yet your heavenly Father feeds them. Are you not of more value than they? Which of you by worrying can add one cubit to his stature? . . . Therefore do not worry about tomorrow, for tomorrow will worry about its own things. Sufficient for the day is its own trouble."

— Matthew 6:25-27, 34

In the movie *The Patriot,* Benjamin Martin is a former soldier who has seen the horrors of war up-close, and been responsible for some pretty horrific acts in the name of God and king. After the death of his wife, he is left to raise his children as a single father. Having left his life as a warrior behind, he is once again thrust into the middle of the American Revolution when it shows up (quite literally) in his front yard. When his young son is gunned down in front of him by the brutal British Colonel Tavington, he makes the decision to fight for the Continental Army, leading a group of renegades on guerilla raids on

THE SERMON

the British regulars. Martin, a man who has already lost much loses much more in the course of the story, which is borne out in the eerily-prophetic opening line of the movie: "I have long feared that my sins would return to visit me, and the cost is more than I can bear." [55]

Whether worrying about your sins "finding you out," or just worrying for no good reason, fear and worry are powerful thing. So, I ask you . . .

Are you a worrier?

Did you know worry is destructive?

Did you know worry is a sin?

However, in the verses that began this chapter, Jesus sets forth the secret to peace of mind. It is the Uncommon Life that knows how to cope with worry. If you look back at the previous section, you can see some of the sources of worry. The idolatry of possessions, position, and profession are often causes of worry. Add to that financial issues, job problems, and family turmoil, and you cover a wide range of sources of worry.

Remember the story of the rich fool? He was worried about where to store his goods. Remember Midas and his golden touch? The thing he thought would make him rich became the touch of death to those around him. What we think we desire and need for success and security will often drive us to worry.

In the *Peanuts* comic strip, Marcie gave good advice to worrier Charlie Brown: "I promise there'll be a tomorrow, sir. In fact, it's already tomorrow in Australia."[56]

You are meant FOR more.

"Therefore I say to you, do not worry about your life, what you will eat or what you will drink; nor about your body, what you will put on."

Make no mistake about it—worry distracts you from your purpose. The phrase "do not worry" literally means "anxious care." Understand that, in the New Testament, there are two kinds of care. Besides anxious care there is also responsible care—care that looks to God for personal and family needs. This concern and diligence is the opposite of laziness.

Jesus condemns anxiety over temporal matters. After you have diligently obeyed the Lord, what more can you do? By worrying over things, we dishonor and disobey God. Matthew 13:22 warns us, *"Now he who received seed among the thorns is he who hears the word, and the cares of this world and the deceitfulness of riches choke the word, and he becomes unfruitful."*

Worry renders the believer unfruitful. Constant grinding worry and anxiety shows an extreme lack of faith in God, and could possibly be a sign that the worrier may not even be saved. By worrying, we short-change our effectiveness, and the ability of God to bless us. As Paul wrote, *"And without faith it is impossible to please God, because anyone who comes to Him must believe that He exists and that He rewards those who earnestly seek Him"* (Hebrews 11:6 NIV).

Faith is one of the linchpins of the Uncommon Life. Faith is a cornerstone of our belief system. Lack of faith is not just a bad idea— it is the main ingredient in a life of mediocrity and failure. The reward system of God is founded and grounded in faith, and the Uncommon Life is impossible without it. Matthew 6:25 reminds us, *"Life is more."*

THE SERMON

Anxiety and worry help to perpetrate the lie that it's not, and derails us from our true purpose while we spend all of our time worrying about and running after the superficial—food, drink, clothing, money, etc. In the end, worry is a thief that robs us of sleep, strength, and true success. This thief distracts us from the promises of God:

Jesus said, *"The thief does not come except to steal, and to kill, and to destroy. I have come that they may have life, and that they may have it more abundantly"* (John 10:10). Jesus came to give you the abundant life, not anxious life. Jesus came to stop the "worry-thief" dead in his tracks; all that it requires is faith on our part.

Think of it like a home-security system. A security system can protect your home from all manner of dangers, including thieves. These systems include motion sensors, door sensors, glass-break sensors, and a variety of other hi-tech indicators. It can notify you immediately in the event of an intrusion. You can have the more impregnable, foolproof security system in the world. However, it is utterly worthless if you never flip the switch and turn it on. Faith is the switch that protects us from the worry-thief, and energizes our spiritual "security system" with the power of the Holy Spirit.

You are meant to DO more.

"Look at the birds of the air, for they neither sow nor reap nor gather into barns; yet your heavenly Father feeds them. Are you not of more value than they?"

Jesus points out that, by nature, animals do not worry. It is only human beings that worry. The same God who has provided for the animals of the forests and seas, clothes the lilies of the field, and follows the flight patterns of birds in the sky will take care of our

MISSION IMPOSSIBLE?

needs. Jesus asked, *"Which of you by worrying can add one cubit to his stature?"* If He were here speaking to us today, He might have said, "Which of you, by worrying, can cause yourself to grow one inch in height, lose one inch around your waist, add one hair to your head, or make yourself one iota stronger?"

Regardless of the century or verbiage, what He is saying here is that worry is useless. Worry changes nothing and produces nothing positive. Worry robs you of the energy, desire, and "faith" resources necessary to fulfill the plan God has for your life. Worry destroys your productivity. Worry does not have the ability to add quality to life; it only diminishes whatever areas of life it touches.

Several years ago, a young businessman I know visited his doctor. He was worn out, and the economic collapse of the economy in 2008 left his already-struggling business in shambles, and his life a stressed-out mess. His doctor repeatedly told him, "You need to cut some of the stress out of your life."

He didn't listen.

He saw no way of cutting back or letting up on his hectic schedule, trying to save his business and provide for his family. He paid little attention to his health, his diet, or his sleep patterns, and often joked about his self-destructive behavior. After a few more years of living this way, he suffered a heart attack

When the surgeon performed the arteriogram to determine whether his situation could be treated with a stent or if he was going to face open-heart surgery, to his amazement, the doctor found nothing wrong—no blockages at all. After this experience, my friend saw this as a "shot across the bow," and changed how he lived. This experience became a faith-builder for him—a second chance from God—and he

THE SERMON

determined to listen, not just to his doctor, but to the Holy Spirit as well. He started exercising and taking better care of his physical body, but also identified the worry-thieves in his life, and changed things dramatically, learning how to turn things over to God. While he would probably admit he still has a long way to go, he told me that finding faith and letting go of worry and stress were huge steps in the right direction.

Stress and worry are killers, and Jesus wants us to be rid of them, once and for all. As we move toward the end of the age, He warns us: *"Take heed to yourselves, lest your hearts be weighed down with carousing, drunkenness, and cares of this life, and that Day come on you unexpectedly. For it will come as a snare on all those who dwell on the face of the whole earth"* (Luke 21:34-35).

You are meant to HAVE more.

"So why do you worry about clothing? Consider the lilies of the field, how they grow: they neither toil nor spin; and yet I say to you that even Solomon in all his glory was not arrayed like one of these. Now if God so clothes the grass of the field, which today is, and tomorrow is thrown into the oven, will He not much more clothe you, O you of little faith?

"Therefore do not worry, saying, 'What shall we eat?' or 'What shall we drink?' or 'What shall we wear?' For after all these things the Gentiles seek. For your heavenly Father knows that you need all these things" (Matthew 6:28-32).

The last phrase of verse 30 pretty well sums it up, *"O you of little faith."*

MISSION IMPOSSIBLE?

- Worry denies the care of God.

- Worry denies the provision of God.

- Worry abandons faith for human reason.

Our heavenly Father knows what we need. This is not about prosperity or an abundance of stuff. He promises here to meet our basic needs. If we don't trust Him to provide for us, how can we trust Him to prosper us? If we don't believe Him for the basic thing, can we really believe Him for the big thing?

Psalm 104 indicates that God has, by nature, ordained the provision of His wild creatures—"living things both small and great. . . . These all wait for You, that You may give them their food in due season" (vv. 25, 27). This should put our culture of worry and anxiety to shame.

"Unless the Lord builds the house, they labor in vain who build it; unless the Lord guards the city, the watchman stays awake in vain. It is vain for you to rise up early, to sit up late, to eat the bread of sorrows; for so He gives His beloved sleep" (Psalm 127:1-2).

This psalm speaks of the variety of our worries. It's not just about what we do, or even our motivation. Seemingly good intentions, if not activated by faith, can ultimately be meaningless. Even "productive" labor, if not subject to God and given to Him by faith, is futile in the end.

"You have sown much, and bring in little;

You eat, but do not have enough;

You drink, but you are not filled with drink;

You clothe yourselves, but no one is warm;

And he who earns wages, earns wages to put into a bag with holes."

THE SERMON

> *Thus says the Lord of hosts: "Consider your ways! Go up to the mountains and bring wood and build the temple, that I may take pleasure in it and be glorified," says the Lord. "You looked for much, but indeed it came to little; and when you brought it home, I blew it away. Why?" says the Lord of hosts. "Because of My house that is in ruins, while every one of you runs to his own house"* (Haggai 1:6-9).

We cannot expect the blessings of God to come to us if we are living in disobedience. In this passage, the people are trying to look after their own needs while neglecting the house of God. While they tried to supply for themselves, Jehovah's house is in shambles. These words declare that we should never worry about our food, fashion, or future at the expense of obedience to the commands of God. When we diligently obey the Lord, His provision will be there for us.

Your Mission Is Possible.

God's Word does not deny the value of human work, as work is a Scriptural concept, and God does not contradict Himself. What the Bible does deny is human worry. So, when all is said and done, what can we do to overcome anxiety and defeat the worry-thief?

> *Rejoice in the Lord always. Again I will say, rejoice! Let your gentleness be known to all men. The Lord is at hand. Be anxious for nothing, but in everything by prayer and supplication, with thanksgiving, let your requests be made known to God; and the peace of God, which surpasses all understanding, will guard your hearts and minds through Christ Jesus* (Philippians 4:4-7).

Living the Uncommon Life is more than possible; it is guaranteed. But that guarantee comes at a cost: letting go and allowing God to take control of the things that keep us wound up tighter than a ten-day clock. I've heard it said that 99 percent of the things we worry about never come to pass. Not only does the enemy want to keep you wound up and bound to anxiety surrounding your real situation, he wants to distract you with fear and worry about situations over which you have absolutely no control whatsoever. That seems to me like a lot of energy wasted on things that amount to nothing—energy that could be better spent fixing our gaze on and moving toward a limitless horizon as one pursuing the Uncommon Life.

I want to end this chapter with a simple formula you can dwell on when you come face-to-face with the worry-thief.

Rejoice: As a believer and potential "Un-commoner," you have God's presence with you.

Request: God knows what you need (actually, before you do). However, as any dutiful Father, He wants you to realize your dependence on Him. He just wants you to ask. You have the power of prayer at your disposal; use it.

Rest: Finding the faith that pleases God opens the pathway to the peace of God—peace that passes all understanding that will keep you safe from the worry-thief.

Are you ready to walk in your new possibility and potential? Are you ready to give up the worry and anxiety of the life of a commoner to take on the mantle of an Un-commoner?

THE SERMON

KEY QUESTIONS TO PONDER
Chapter 15: *Mission Impossible?*

1. Jesus said *"Do not worry about your life."* Since God promises to take care of us, why do so many Christians worry?

2. Why is worry a destructive habit? What does worry do: physically? mentally? spiritually?

3. Read Philippians 4:4-7. Discuss how to apply these verses to our everyday walk with the Lord.

Chapter 16
IN SEARCH OF . . .
The Life that Lives with God's Priorities

"For after all these things the Gentiles seek. For your heavenly Father knows that you need all these things. But seek first the kingdom of God and His righteousness, and all these things shall be added to you."

—Matthew 6:32-33

A few years ago, the Powerball lottery game going on in several states hit an all-time high jackpot: over $1.5 billion. In the days prior to hitting that mark, it was reported to be at $800 million, and because of the furor over the projected payout, it jumped hundreds of millions of dollars over the next few days. One very lucky person stood to become a billionaire (before taxes) overnight. Of course, statistically speaking, you would have a better chance of being struck by lightning while simultaneously being sworn in as President of the United States than of winning the big prize.

Remember the saying "Get all you can, can all you get, and sit on the lid"? For that one person (or even two or three), that would take a very big can. But most people who become instantly rich already have a shopping list of all of the stuff they plan to buy with their newfound wealth. Cars, homes, boats, travel, and a wide assortment of expensive

THE SERMON

toys usually top the list. Maybe that is why, in many cases, people who win vast sums of money end up in bankruptcy court within a few years.

Individuals are seeking after stuff. Governments and nations are seeking after stuff as well. However, the Uncommon Life seeks after the things of God. God is first in the lives of those who will truly make a positive, long-lasting difference in this world. But making God's priorities our priorities doesn't just happen. It takes discipline and seeking after Him.

If God's priorities are to be ours, then we must seek Him in four ways.

1. RELATIONSHIP

"For your heavenly Father knows that you need all these things."

Notice that God is referred to as your "heavenly Father." To know God is to know Him as our "Daddy God." Maybe your experience with your earthly father was less than it should have been, and the only father you have ever known was abusive, manipulative, emotionally distant, or physically absent. Maybe the thought of a loving daddy is a foreign concept to you. You can rest assured that your heavenly Father is kind, loving, merciful, and gracious. He is a Father who will never leave, never abandon, never abuse, and never disappoint. His love is everlasting, and His faithfulness is without equal.

So how do we enter into a relationship with such a Father? Any relationship with God starts with a relationship with Jesus. In John 14:6, Jesus said, *"I am the Way, the Truth, and the Life. No one comes to the Father except through Me."*

When we open the door of our hearts to Jesus, He turns the tables, and opens the door to the throne room of Heaven to us. Acceptance of Him grants us instant access to the presence of God: *"He who has seen Me has seen the Father"* (John 14:9).

When we come to Jesus, we are born again, and can now experience the invisible Kingdom of God in the here and now. We can approach His presence with confidence that our Father has our best interests at heart, even the seemingly little stuff.

In May 2002, I was preaching a crusade in Nigeria. After about a week of wonderful meetings, it was time to once again climb aboard a plane and head back across the Atlantic. As we were about to leave, we were praying with our host pastor, Dr. Nick Ezeh, and rejoicing in what God had done in the meetings. After saying our goodbyes, we turned and walked into the terminal only to be confronted by these disturbing words on the flight schedule screen: Flight #— to Lagos: CANCELLED!

Now, in the U.S., this is not really a huge issue. When a flight is cancelled, most of the time, there is another flight within hours. However, since we were in Calabar, Nigeria, and not Cleveland, Ohio, this was not the case. If we missed our connection in Lagos, the next available flight was four days later!

At this point, our team shifted into overdrive, trying desperately to speak to someone who might have a solution to our dilemma. We quickly discovered there was a flight to Lagos from another town called Port Harcourt. The flight was scheduled to leave in three hours and forty-five minutes. Great, right? Except for one small problem— Port Harcourt was more than three hours away.

If we left immediately, we would have a fifteen-minute margin of error. If we hit traffic, had any mechanical issues, or were in any other way delayed, chances were good that we would not make our

THE SERMON

connection, and would have to get comfortable for a four-day layover. Our team quickly gathered all of our gear, and got back into the vehicles for the long ride to Port Harcourt.

Now, one thing about Nigeria is that twice a year they shut down all of the oil refineries for a week or two for scheduled maintenance, thus creating shortages, rationing, and gas-station shutdowns all over the country. It just so happened that a shutdown fell during our visit. The whole time we were there, we witnessed lines at gas stations that made the U.S. gas lines of the 1970s look like the express line at Wal-Mart. About an hour into our drive, I glanced down at the gas gauge of our borrowed vehicle, and noticed the needle was below empty. Our driver, a very nice Nigerian gentleman by the name of A. G. Bright, didn't seem too concerned. I leaned forward and asked him if the gauge was broken.

"No, my brother," he answered, "but God will provide, for we prayed for mercy on this journey. Also, you and Dr. Ezeh are God's men. He will surely see us through."

It is difficult to admit this, but my faithless soul was not comforted. As we drove on, my mind was filled with visions of our stranded team, standing by our vehicles in the middle of the sweltering Nigerian jungle, or worse, being taken captive by rebels or robbers.

As my mind raced through the worst possible of scenarios, all of a sudden, I heard the sound of singing. Mr. Bright had started singing praises to God, and was quickly being joined by others in the vehicle. As the praises went up from our SUV, my faithless heart still continued to fret, expecting our engine to come to a grinding halt at any second. However, after another hour of unrelenting driving, we came to a crossroads, with a gas station that stood like an oasis at the intersection. As we pulled in, we questioned whether or not it was even open, since it was without the massive lines we had witnessed everywhere else. Upon discovering it was open, we soon found out from the proprietor that the station had been closed for a week due to the fuel shortage, but that he had just received a shipment, and was actually re-opening his station as we pulled up!

A smiling A. G. Bright looked at me and said, "See, Pastor Phillips. God always takes care of His servants. You are in favor with God!"

Now nearly two decades later, we face challenges like never before. Turmoil in our financial markets, uncertainty and unrest about the state of our nation politically, and chaos and disquiet in various hot-spots around the globe make it difficult to have faith. Yet having the favor of God is not dependent upon who is king, prime minister, or president. The favor of God does not hinge on "bull markets" or diversified portfolios. The favor of God is not even affected by our immediate circumstances—our job, our family, or even our gas gauge. The favor of God is about His goodness and faithfulness to His children. It is about that Father/child relationship. It is about having access to "every good and perfect gift" that comes from His throne to His children with "no shadow of turning." We receive God's favor not because we are good, but because He is good.

Driving down those dirty, pot-hole infested roads of Nigeria that day, Mr. Bright became a shining example of how we get ahold of that favor.

Mr. Bright prayed, knowing whose child he was. He prayed a prayer that said, "My Father, here is what I am expecting, and no one will be more surprised than me if You don't come through." (Contrast this with the prayer that many of us pray: "God, here is my need, and I will be shocked if You actually answer me.")

THE SERMON

Mr. Bright walked by faith. He put his proverbial "money where his mouth was." He had no choice but to move forward by faith, and he did it with gusto, literally driving into the unknown with nothing but a belief that God is true to His Word and to His children.

Mr. Bright worshipped; he didn't sit there and fret about the gas gauge. He opened his mouth and declared God's goodness and faithfulness in advance.

What a powerful lesson! I want to be like Mr. Bright. I want to be the one who walks in favor, stands in favor, and lives in favor. I want to be the one whose life is centered in a relationship that puts me in the presence of the Father, and in the blessing God gave Moses for the children of Israel: *"The Lord bless you and keep you; the Lord make his face shine on you and be gracious to you; the Lord turn his face toward you and give you peace"* (Numbers 6:24-27 NIV).

Moreover, because of this relationship with the Father, it makes me a brother to all who know Him as Father. As a child of the Father, I am now in an enormous, diverse, many-colored, multilingual, ageless, eternal family. While we can collectively call Him "Our Father," we as individuals can each approach Him as "my Father." Furthermore, being a child of the Father, I can have a "much more" life by the Holy Spirit. Jesus said, *"If you then, being evil, know how to give good gifts to your children, how much more will your heavenly Father give the Holy Spirit to those who ask Him!"* (Luke 11:13).

When the Holy Spirit brings me into the family of God, He cries out, *"Abba, Father"* (Galatians 4:6), and I cry back "Abba, Father": *"For you did not receive the spirit of bondage again to fear, but you received the Spirit of adoption by whom we cry out, 'Abba, Father'"* (Romans 8:15).

This confession keeps you from shrinking the immensity of the Kingdom into your tiny box of tradition, denomination, pet doctrine, race, style, age, musical preference, political ideology, or country of origin. When it came to resolving difficult issues, the early church relied upon the creed of Scripture, not "hair-splitting," to settle these matters.

> *They drew a circle that shut me out*
>
> *A rebel, a heretic, a thing to flout!*
>
> *But love and I had the will to win,*
>
> *We drew a circle that took Him in.* [57]

2. REIGN

"Seek first the Kingdom of God."

When I come to Jesus, I enter a Kingdom, and choose to live under His reign. Colossians 1:13-14 says, *"He has delivered us from the power of darkness and conveyed us into the kingdom of the Son of His love, in whom we have redemption through His blood, the forgiveness of sins."*

- *His Kingdom is large.* It includes all who come to Jesus.

- *His Kingdom is living.* There is always growth where His Kingdom operates. There will be movement, birth, growth, noise, increase, and glory when He is King.

- *His Kingdom is lasting.* It had no beginning, and will have no end.

He is King of Kings!

THE SERMON

3. RIGHTEOUSNESS

"Seek . . . His righteousness."

When you look for a description of *God's Kingdom*, you find one given by Paul in Romans. He declared, *"For the kingdom of God is not eating and drinking, but righteousness and peace and joy in the Holy Spirit"* (Romans 14:17).

Now clearly, righteousness is not of our works. Righteousness only comes in the person of Jesus Christ. *"But of Him you are in Christ Jesus, who became for us wisdom from God—and righteousness and sanctification and redemption"* (1 Corinthians 1:30).

"Therefore let no one boast in men. For all things are yours: whether Paul or Apollos or Cephas, or the world or life or death, or things present or things to come—all are yours. And you are Christ's, and Christ is God's" (3:21-23).

Righteousness is the gift of God to us. It is not something we can work for or earn. It is a spiritual shift that elevates us from a pauper in the back alleys of humankind to royalty in the Kingdom. *"For if by the one man's offense death reigned through the one, much more those who receive abundance of grace and of the gift of righteousness will reign in life through the One, Jesus Christ"* (Romans 5:17).

The Holy Spirit applies and activates this righteousness as a force in your life: *"And if Christ is in you, the body is dead because of sin, but the Spirit is life because of righteousness"* (Romans 8:10).

Therefore, when you do sin, God does not cast you out; instead, He chastens you: *"Now no chastening seems to be joyful for the present, but painful; nevertheless, afterward it yields the peaceable fruit of righteousness to those who have been trained by it"* (Hebrews 12:11).

Chastening and correction are never pleasant, but God chastens His children for their betterment. If you are a child of the Father, then His righteousness, born out of correction, will once again bring forth fruit in your life. Believers have the righteousness of Christ, which empowers them as Christ works righteousness and peace through them. *"Little children, let no one deceive you. He who practices righteousness is righteous, just as He is righteous"* (1 John 3:7).

Here's a great way to look at it: Righteousness is the right conduct of God expressed through those who are children of the Kingdom.

4. REWARD

"And all these things shall be added to you."

Money, food, drink, clothing all the things named in Matthew 6 are what the world is after. These are the things they are competing, beating, cheating, and killing each other for. But provision—God's provision— is a byproduct of putting our heavenly Father, His will, and His purposes first in our lives. In fact, the word *added* translates *prostithem* (Greek), which means "to increase." Not only will God supply your needs, but He will give you added provision. *"For the Lord God is a sun and shield; the Lord will give grace and glory; no good thing will He withhold from those who walk uprightly"* (Psalm 84:11).

As a young preacher, I spent quite a bit of time living in and around New Orleans. I went to seminary there, as well as pastored there. If there is one thing I know about the people of Louisiana, they are a generous people. It is customary in Louisiana to give more than asked or ordered. If you are in a bakery, and buy a dozen items, more often than not, the proprietor will give you thirteen. This is called

THE SERMON

"lagniappe." So why should it surprise us that our Father wants to give us more, and that He desires to go above and beyond our expectations? He does, you know? That is just the kind of God we love and serve!

So, have you found what you are searching for?

The Uncommon Life recognizes a good deal when it sees it. One of the greatest illustrations in the Bible is the parable of the pearl of great price. Jesus said, *"The kingdom of heaven is like a merchant seeking beautiful pearls, who, when he had found one pearl of great price, went and sold all that he had and bought it"* (Matthew 13:45-46).

Here is one who sought the best, and when he found it, recognized its surpassing wealth, and spared no expense to own it. He gave everything he had in order to have it. Yet in finding it, he received all.

> *"I lost it all*
> *To find everything*
> *I died a pauper*
> *To be born a king!"* [58]

KEY QUESTIONS TO PONDER
Chapter 16: *In Search of...*

1. Read Matthew 6:33 and discuss its meaning in light of the admonition, "Take no thought of your life."

2. How are we supposed to "seek" the Kingdom? Is this a suggestion or a command? When a material need arises is seeking "God's Kingdom first" a challenge for you? Do you try to figure it out on your own? Discuss.

3. Read Colossians 1:13-14. What is the meaning of the phrase, *"the kingdom of the Son of His love"*? What were we delivered from? What where we delivered to?

Chapter 17
Judgment Day
The Life that Takes Off the Mask

"Judge not, that you be not judged. For with what judgment you judge, you will be judged; and with the measure you use, it will be measured back to you. And why do you look at the speck in your brother's eye, but do not consider the plank in your own eye? Or how can you say to your brother, 'Let me remove the speck from your eye'; and look, a plank is in your own eye? Hypocrite! First remove the plank from your own eye, and then you will see clearly to remove the speck from your brother's eye."

—Matthew 7:1-5

One of the phenomena of our modern culture is "reality television." From competitive reality shows such as *American Idol*, *The Apprentice*, *The Voice*, and *Survivor* to "life under the lens" shows such as *The Simple Life*, *The Real Housewives*, and *Keeping Up with The Kardashians*, there are literally hundreds of reality shows from which to choose. One has only to do an online search of "reality shows" to be completely overwhelmed with program after program from every conceivable borough and bent. Upon doing my own online search when writing this, it revealed over 860 different programs—that was the point at which I stopped counting.

THE SERMON

The problem with "reality" programming is that, for the majority of us, this is *not* reality. Most of us get up in the morning, work a solid eight-hour day for (probably) less than we deserve, without fanfare, accolades, or bravado. We try to abide by the laws, live within our means, pay our bills and taxes on time, and find our happiness in our faith, families, and communities. I find it amazing that, for a generation and culture fixated on being "real," we have become obsessed with television programming that is anything but real. When your toughest decision of the day is cappuccino or macchiato, Armani or Oscar de la Renta, or "Should I lay around my pool all day?" or "Should I treat myself to a full-body massage?" . . . that's not a "reality" most of us can relate to.

One of the marks of the Uncommon Life is the ability to be real. In Matthew 7:1-5, we find the word *hypocrite*, which we also found in chapter 6. It is the idea of pretending to be something you are not. The passage before us deals with those who judge others while hiding behind a mask. If we take off the mask, the one judging is as bad (or worse) as the one he has condemned. As a pastor, I have seen this kind of deception and misdirection over and over again in local churches, as well as on the national stage: One person falls to sin, and the vultures swoop in. In many cases, the one with the loudest, most judgmental voice is guilty of the same or worse. They ignore the adage, "Those who live in glass houses should not throw stones." It is usually just a matter of time before they are uncovered for their hypocrisy, and are publicly humiliated. As we unfold this passage in Matthew 7, we will clear up much of the misunderstanding we have about judgment, and will be encouraged to live authentic lives; becoming agents not of judgment, but of salvation.

These verses concern passing judgment on your fellow believers. This passage has been sorely misused across the centuries. People often use it as an excuse to be left alone in their sin. Honestly, such misquoting has gotten us to the place we are in our society; we have nearly lost the ability to say something is wrong for fear of being called judgmental. Such misunderstanding, combined with the "politically correct" atmosphere of our culture, puts us standing on perilously thin ice. In this chapter, we will attempt to put these verses in their proper context, gain some understanding, and get back on solid ground with regard to our understanding of judgment.

HONEST JUDGMENT

"Judge not, that you be not judged."

The misapplication of Matthew 7:1 could, in some people's minds, give us an argument for the dissolution of our entire judicial system. After all, if we are not to judge each other in *any* instance, then who is to say what is right and wrong? What makes telling the truth admirable, and stealing a crime? What makes the actions of people like Adolph Hitler, Pol Pot, and Osama bin Laden abhorrent? After all, if they were merely doing what they deemed to be right, what gives us the right to judge?

Think *context.*

If believers are commanded not to judge each other with certain attitudes, obviously, there must be a correct and honest judgment. This passage does not condemn the critical faculty God has given us to discern right from wrong. Jesus teaches us to "judge" who are our brothers, who are "false prophets," and which way is the "narrow way." This command does not mean we suspend our abilities to discern right from wrong, or good conduct from evil conduct.

Here the command obviously has to do with a vigilante spirit. It

THE SERMON

has to do not so much with judging acts, but with questioning motives and sincerity. Several passages commend honest judgment.

Luke 12:57 says, *"Why, even of yourselves, do you not judge what is right?"*

John 7:24 instructs us to *"judge with righteous judgment."*

Hebrews 5:14 tells us we are to have our *"senses exercised to discern both good and evil."*

Here are three lawful and honest judgments:

1. *Civil Judgment (Romans 13):* The Word of God provides for the judging of criminals in our society.

2. *Spiritual Judgment (Matthew 18):* Church discipline is taught clearly in the Word of God. The church has the authority to judge in matters of faith, conduct, and fellowship (Galatians 5; 1 Corinthians 5).

3. *Scriptural Judgment (2 Timothy 3 and 4):* The preacher and teacher, within the bounds of the Word of God, stand under a direct command to "convince, rebuke, and exhort." Furthermore, they are to declare the "whole counsel of God." To share the judgments of God's Word is not to offend.

HARSH JUDGMENT

"For with what judgment you judge, you will be judged; and with the measure you use, it will be measured back to you."

It is the harsh and unlawful judgment of a fellow Christian that is condemned in Matthew 7:2. We find here the spirit of the fault-finder, the nit-picker, and the bean-counter in full force; always looking for the inconsistencies and failings in others. This individual always questions the motives, pours cold water on the plans, and is unforgiving toward the mistakes of others. Let's take a look at several truths about when it is wrong to judge:

1. *It is wrong to judge another when it is outside your responsibility.* Paul asked: *"Who are you to judge another's servant? To his own master he stands or falls. Indeed, he will be made to stand, for God is able to make him stand"* (Romans 14:4).

This verse declares it is before one's master that a servant stands or falls. Criticism, instruction, and discipline are a master's responsibility, not ours. A master sets the standard for his servant; that responsibility is given to them by God, not to us.

2. *It is wrong to judge prematurely.* Second Corinthians 4:4-5 says: *"For I know of nothing against myself, yet I am not justified by this; but He who judges me is the Lord. Therefore judge nothing before the time, until the Lord comes, who will both bring to light the hidden things of darkness and reveal the counsels of the hearts. Then each one's praise will come from God."*

The motives of a person's heart are known only by God, even more so than by the man himself. We can't know what is in another person's heart. The Lord will reveal at His coming the worth of the works and motives of others.

3. *It is wrong to judge another person presumptuously.* This happens when you accept hearsay and rumor, and pass judgment on the conduct of others. As a pastor for many years, I have seen reputations ruined, careers trashed, marriages crumble, and lives destroyed because of careless judgment.

4. *It is wrong to judge hastily.* God the Father, who sees and know all, still renders no judgment without investigation and fact. When people took it upon themselves to construct the Tower of Babel, the

THE SERMON

Bible says, *"But the Lord came down to see the city and the tower which the sons of men had built"* (Genesis 11:5).

A few chapters later, the Lord says this with regard to the reputation and sin of the people of Sodom and Gomorrah: *"I will go down now and see whether they have done altogether according to the outcry against it that has come to Me; and if not, I will know"* (18:21).

So, if the God of the universe who sees all from His throne still chooses to come down and investigate human affairs, and witness first-hand the actions of His creation, who are we to pass hasty judgment without investigation, empirical facts, and testimony of our own eyes?

Proverbs 18:13 says, *"He who answers a matter before he hears it, It is folly and shame to him."* In John 7:24, Jesus said, *"Do not judge according to appearance, but judge with righteous judgment."*

5. *It is wrong to judge personally.* Often, one will judge others on the basis of his own personal convictions. Whether celebrities, political candidates, sports figures, or the guy four houses down the street, we all too often judge the actions of others by the high standard of our own personal belief system and convictions. With celebrities, we want them to be the same superhero we see them play on the screen; the one we aspire to be ourselves. For politics, we are looking for the ideal candidate, who sees eye-to-eye with us on every single issue. In sports, we want the guy on the field that excels at all he does, and breaks every record to be the same role model off the field. We want the guy down the street to have the same respect for the law, the neighborhood, and his own lawn that we believe we embody. The fact is that, in most cases, we are asking others to live up to a standard that not even we live up to.

In Romans 14, Paul warns us of those who judge the personal actions of others. In Colossians 2, he again warns us of the bondage of human laws: *"Therefore, if you died with Christ from the basic principles of the world, why, as though living in the world, do you subject yourselves to regulations—'Do not touch, do not taste, do not handle,' which all concern things which perish with the using—according to the commandments and doctrines of men? These things indeed have an appearance of wisdom in self-imposed religion, false humility, and neglect of the body, but are of no value against the indulgence of the flesh"* (vv. 20-23).

6. *It is wrong to judge unmercifully.* To condemn another without the hope of pardon is wrong. A graphic illustration of wrong judgment is found in 2 Samuel 10, when David sent servants to King Hanun of Ammon to comfort him on the death of his father. Hanun was persuaded by false witnesses that David's emissaries had evil motives. Judgment was passed on David's men, the result of which was a horrible war. As this story bore out, when we misjudge the motives and attitudes of others, it can lead to disastrous results.

HYPOCRITICAL JUDGMENT

"And why do you look at the speck in your brother's eye, but do not consider the plank in your own eye?"

Jesus says the one doing the judging is worse than the one on being judged. In the attempt to get the splinter out of someone else's eye, this person is ignoring the 2-by-12 in his own eye. The fact is, no one is in any shape to censor another if that person has unconfessed sin and unresolved guilt in their own life. *"Brethren, if a man is overtaken in any trespass, you who are spiritual restore such a one in a spirit of gentleness, considering yourself lest you also be tempted"* (Galatians 6:1).

THE SERMON

Only the spiritual person is to restore. Paul instructs the Galatians to allow "you who are spiritual" to take the fallen through the process of restoration.

"Restore in a spirit of meekness and humility." Those who restore must recognize their own weakness and frailty.

Being a "restorer" is conditional. A person should commit to helping restore another individual only if they realistically understand the weakness of their own flesh, and the fact that they could be subject to similar temptations.

Only a cleansed people can exercise proper discipline. It becomes a sad reproach when the carnal are permitted to condemn each other.

One of the worst church fights I ever saw took place when some carnal men tried to keep another carnal man from being elected to the deacon board. Criticism for past failures were brought up, and all of the families involved ended up leaving the church over the incident. The church was wounded, people were hurt, and the cause of Christ was shamed by the actions of people who claimed to love Him, but failed to love each other.

HELPUL JUDGMENT

"Hypocrite! First remove the plank from your own eye, and then you will see clearly to remove the speck from your brother's eye."

Can you imagine having a person trying to remove a small speck of dust from your eye, all the while having a huge wooden beam protruding from his own eye? The visual of this seems pretty absurd, but that is the picture Jesus is drawing in Matthew 7:5. The proper way to help a brother overcome his shortcomings is to first remove the very thing that is going to keep you from seeing clearly. You have to make sure you are personally right with God before you presume to correct someone else. When your heart is clean and your motives are pure, you are in a position to correct and help someone else who is wrong or struggling. It is this state of heart that enables us to restore and rescue a brother or sister.

And with this Word comes a warning: At the Judgment, we will be judged based on how we judged others (v. 2). The standard we use to point out and judge the faults of others will be applied to us when we stand before God. If we enjoy occupying the bench as judge, we cannot plead ignorance of the law we wrongly try to administer. *"Therefore you are inexcusable, O man, whoever you are who judge, for in whatever you judge another you condemn yourself; for you who judge practice the same things"* (Romans 2:1).

We are inexcusable if we judge others. We are recipients of grace and mercy; they should characterize our lives. Any lawyer will tell you that ignorance of the law is not a defense against prosecution and penalty; it is much less so for the person who sits in judgment, creating an illusion of righteousness, all the while being as guilty as the accused. However, God wants to set you free from, well, yourself. If you will get off the critic's seat, God can set you free to love others as they are, and in the process, become an agent of healing, reconciliation, love, and restoration.

Chrysostom, the great preacher of the 3rd century, said this of the sinning brother: "Correct him, but not as a foe or adversary exacting a penalty, but as a physician providing medicine." If we will heed this wisdom, I believe we will see God heal and restore the relationships of His feuding children.

THE SERMON

KEY QUESTIONS TO PONDER
Chapter 17: *Judgment Day*

1. Jesus said, *"Judge not, that you be not judged."* What does He mean? Are we to do away with our entire judicial system since we are told not to judge anyone?

2. List three areas of lawful and honest judgments:

_____ Judgment (Romans 13)

_____ Judgment (Matthew 18)

_____ Judgment (2 Timothy 3-4)

3. Read Galatians 6:1. Why aren't we seeing more "spiritual restoration" today in the body of Christ? Who is qualified to "restore" a fallen brother?

Chapter 18
IS NOTHING SACRED?

The Life that Respects the Sacred

"Do not give what is holy to the dogs; nor cast your pearls before swine, lest they trample them under their feet, and turn and tear you in pieces."—Matthew 7:6

He who corrects a scoffer gets shame for himself, and he who rebukes a wicked man only harms himself. Do not correct a scoffer, lest he hate you; rebuke a wise man, and he will love you.

—Proverbs 9:7-8

The election cycle of 2016 was one of the most vicious political seasons in American history. Social media played a huge role (good or bad) in the distribution of information (good and bad) about the candidates, their respective positions, and even history itself. One of the presidential candidates ran on a platform that included a call to end the political correctness that has taken a deep foothold in our nation. This political correctness has—in the interest of justifying the moral, social, and political positions of some—attempted to revise our very history. And while the world witnessed the rise of ISIS in the Middle East, and the destruction and desecration of historical sites and centuries of history at the hands of these barbarians in places

THE SERMON

like Timbuktu, Palmyra, Hatra, and many others, Americans have sat in awkward silence at the denigration and dismantling of our own history. As the late U.S. Senator Daniel Patrick Moynihan once said, "Everyone is entitled to his own opinion, but not to his own facts."[59]

If you read the previous five verses of Matthew 7, but miss verse 6, you would completely misunderstand the words of Jesus. While we are commanded not to judge each other wrongly, there is such a thing as spiritual discernment. Truthfully, we use discernment (and dare I say, discrimination) in our everyday lives on a nearly continual basis. Simple acts—choosing what to wear, where to eat lunch, what kind of car to drive—all require a degree of discernment (and discrimination). When you choose to not eat at a restaurant that was rated poorly by the health department, you are "discerning" that eating at such an establishment may not be in your best interest. When you choose not to take a side in an argument at work, it may be because you are discerning that to do so might not be in your best interest. If you choose one brand of peanut butter over another, that is a form of discrimination. Without healthy discernment, there would be a lack of decency and standards, both in the church as well as in society. Without the balancing of truth we find in verse 6, heresy would be rampant, and holiness would be a joke.

In today's society, it seems the only thing wrong is to expose wrong. We have seen this time and again that, when someone is accused of wrongdoing, those in defense of the accused begin to attack the one bringing the allegation.

In an interview with Barbara Walters in the aftermath of the trial of O. J. Simpson, Simpson's attorney Robert Shapiro said, "Not only did we play the race card, we dealt it from the bottom of the deck."

When Walters pointed out the treatment by Shapiro's co-counsel, Johnnie Cochran, of prosecution witness Detective Mark Fuhrman (whom Cochran compared to Hitler), Shapiro replied: "I was deeply offended. To me, the Holocaust stands alone as the most horrible human event in modern civilization, and with the Holocaust comes Adolph Hitler. [And] to compare this man in any way to a rogue cop, in my opinion, was wrong." [60]

We are a civilization of laws. Regardless of personal agendas, accusations, or mudslinging, if a law has been broken, that is the issue that truly matters. Simply stating the laws (of men or God) is not, in and of itself, being what many refer to as "judgmental." It is possible to be discerning without being censorious or viewing ourselves as the final arbiter of judgment.

The language in Matthew 7:6 is blunt. Jesus refers to some in the human family as dogs, and others as swine. Dogs in that day were not the domesticated creatures we see now. They were wild and fierce scavengers. In Jerusalem, they lived primarily in Gehenna, the city garbage dump, where they fought over dead carcasses and waste. Swine in the Hebrew mind stood for all that was filthy, unclean, and outside the norm. "That which is holy" and "pearls" represented truth and the life lived according to the truth. That over which God has made us guardians, His gifts and His truth, are not suitable for every audience.

Shockingly, we see in Jesus' approach to people a contrast. He is kind but direct with the woman at the well, yet he rebukes the Pharisees (see John 4 and Matthew 23). He speaks to Pilate who, as a Roman, did not know the truth, yet Jesus remained silent before Herod who, as a Jew, should have known better (see Matthew 27 and Luke 23).

THE SERMON

There is a time to give and to speak, and there is a time to withhold and be silent.

A WONDERFUL OFFER—GIFTS AND PEARLS

The implication here is that we who know the Lord have something of value to give or offer. God has given us treasure we are encouraged to give away to others. These "pearls" are the Kingdom and all its benefits.

Matthew 13:45-46 reinforces this image: *"Again, the kingdom of heaven is like a merchant seeking beautiful pearls, who, when he had found one pearl of great price, went and sold all that he had and bought it."*

In Revelation 21:21, we see the description of the gateway to Heaven: *"The twelve gates were twelve pearls: each individual gate was of one pearl. And the street of the city was pure gold, like transparent glass."*

Our time, our money, and our abilities are to be given to and given for those who are looking for a better life and a better world. We have life, health, hope, joy, love, power, encouragement, family, and fellowship to offer.

A PASSING OPPORTUNITY—DOGS AND SWINE

There comes a point when the gifts of the Spirit and "the pearl of great price" should not be offered. There are those who have determined and decided to ignore God and His Word. To them, the truth of God is a joke. There are those who have given away their day of grace. They regard our precious treasure as trash. There are those who have given themselves to the world, the flesh, and the devil; God calls them "reprobates."

224

Dogs represent hateful and damaging talk.

"'But against none of the children of Israel shall a dog move its tongue, against man or beast, that you may know that the Lord does make a difference between the Egyptians and Israel'" (Exodus 11:7).

"You therefore, O Lord God of hosts, the God of Israel, awake to punish all the nations; do not be merciful to any wicked transgressors. Selah. At evening they return, they growl like a dog, and go all around the city. Indeed, they belch with their mouth; swords are in their lips; for they say, 'Who hears?' But You, O Lord, shall laugh at them; You shall have all the nations in derision" (Psalm 59:5-8).

Dogs represent immorality.

"You shall not bring the wages of a harlot or the price of a dog to the house of the Lord your God for any vowed offering, for both of these are an abomination to the Lord your God" (Deuteronomy 23:18).

Dogs represent demonic power.

"Deliver Me from the sword, my precious life from the power of the dog" (Psalm 22:20).

Dogs represent the flesh—undisciplined and unsatisfied.

"And at evening they return, they growl like a dog, and go all around the city. They wander up and down for food, and howl if they are not satisfied. But I will sing of Your power; yes, I will sing aloud of Your mercy in the morning; for You have been my defense and refuge in the day of my trouble. To You, O my Strength, I will sing praises; for God is my defense, my God of mercy" (Psalm 59:14-17).

THE SERMON

Dogs represent those who abandon God.

"*As a dog returns to his own vomit, so a fool repeats his folly*" (Proverbs 26:11).

"*While they promise them liberty, they themselves are slaves of corruption; for by whom a person is overcome, by him also he is brought into bondage. For if, after they have escaped the pollutions of the world through the knowledge of the Lord and Savior Jesus Christ, they are again entangled in them and overcome, the latter end is worse for them than the beginning. For it would have been better for them not to have known the way of righteousness, than having known it, to turn from the holy commandment delivered to them. But it has happened to them according to the true proverb: 'A dog returns to his own vomit,' and, 'a sow, having washed, to her wallowing in the mire'*" (2 Peter 2:19-22).

Dogs represent religious form without power.

"*Beware of dogs, beware of evil workers, beware of the mutilation! For we are the circumcision, who worship God in the Spirit, rejoice in Christ Jesus, and have no confidence in the flesh*" (Philippians 3:2-3).

Dogs represent those whom God has given up as reprobates.

"*But outside are dogs and sorcerers and sexually immoral and murderers and idolaters, and whoever loves and practices a lie*" (Revelation 22:15).

Swine represent that which is rotting and dead.

"*And the swine, though it divides the hoof, having cloven hooves, yet does not chew the cud, is unclean to you*" (Leviticus 11:7).

"*Also the swine is unclean for you, because it has cloven hooves, yet does not chew the cud; you shall not eat their flesh or touch their dead carcasses"* (Deuteronomy 14:8).

Swine represent the demon-controlled.

"Now a large herd of swine was feeding there near the mountains. So all the demons begged Him, saying, 'Send us to the swine, that we may enter them.' And at once Jesus gave them permission. Then the unclean spirits went out and entered the swine (there were about two thousand); and the herd ran violently down the steep place into the sea, and drowned in the sea. So those who fed the swine fled, and they told it in the city and in the country. And they went out to see what it was that had happened. Then they came to Jesus, and saw the one who had been demon-possessed and had the legion, sitting and clothed and in his right mind. And they were afraid. And those who saw it told them how it happened to him who had been demon-possessed, and about the swine" (Mark 5:11-16).

Swine represent the filthy dwelling place of the backslider.

"Then he went and joined himself to a citizen of that country, and he sent him into his fields to feed swine. And he would gladly have filled his stomach with the pods that the swine ate, and no one gave him anything" (Luke 15:15-16).

A SAD OUTCOME

While we as believers in the grace of God like to believe no one is beyond His saving grace, the Bible is clear there are those times God allows individuals to be turned over for judgment. *Reprobate* is the term for those God has given up. Three times in Romans 1:20-32, God gives them up. Here are the symptoms and signs of those who have been given up by God:

THE SERMON

So according to this passage, we find the symptoms and signs of those who have been given up by God:

- Deniers of God's glory (v. 21)

- Unthankful (v. 21)

- Arrogant (v. 22)

- Idolaters (v. 23)

- Lustful, immoral (v. 24)

- Lesbianism (v. 26)

- Homosexuality (v. 27)

- Debased thinking (v. 28)

- Unrighteous (v. 29)

- Sexually immoral (v. 29)

- Wicked (v. 29)

- Covetous (v. 29)

- Malicious (v. 29)

- Envious (v. 29)

- Murderers (v. 29)

- Strife—angry and bitter (v. 29)

- Deceitful (v. 29)

- Evil-minded (v. 29)

- Gossips and backbiters (vv. 29-30)

- Haters of God—atheists (v. 30)

- Violent (v. 30)

IS NOTHING SACRED?

- Proud (v. 30)

- Boastful—conceited (v. 30)

- Inventors of evil things (v. 30)

- Disobedient to parents—rebellious (v. 30)

- Not discerning (v. 31)

- Not trustworthy (v. 31)

- Unloving (v. 31)

- Unforgiving (v. 31)

- Unmerciful (v. 31)

- Willfully defiant (v. 32)

- Condoning of those who do the same (v. 32).

When I look at this list, I it strikes closer to home than most of us would care to admit. While some of these things most of us consider "big sins" (murder, wickedness, violence, homosexuality, etc.), in God's view, they carry equal weight. That means to be *unforgiving, proud,* or *unthankful* is as egregious as the "big sins." Kind of sobering, isn't it?

In Titus 1:16, Paul warns of phonies in our midst: *"They profess that they know God; but in works they deny him, being abominable, and disobedient, and unto every good work reprobate"* (KJV).

In the last chapter of the Bible, the Apostle John is told of the moment when it is too late to change: *"And he said to me, 'Do not seal the words of the prophecy of this book, for the time is at hand. He who is unjust, let him be unjust still; he who is filthy, let him be filthy still; he who is righteous, let him be righteous still; he who is holy, let him be holy still'"* (Revelation 22:10-11).

229

THE SERMON

Let me explain this in simple terms. There comes a time when someone . . .

- can live wrong so long they think it is normal

- believes a lie so long they think it is truth

- goes so far they can't get home.

There is a point when the lost become "dogs and swine." They cannot hear the truth. They cannot discern wisdom from folly. They cannot distinguish between the palace of God's holiness and the pigpen of their self-indulgent destruction. In response to the gentle prompting of the Holy Spirit of God, all they can do is bark and blaspheme.

However, God is the only One who can determine how far is too far. God is the only One who can see into people's hearts. We are encouraged to pray and share our faith. We should always remember it is God's grace and kindness that leads people to repentance (Romans 2:4), of which we should be willing vessels.

KEY QUESTIONS TO PONDER
Chapter 18: *Is Nothing Sacred?*

1. Read Matthew 7:6. Was Jesus being too harsh when He compared some people to dogs, and others to swine? What do you think He was talking about? How could you re-phrase this scripture?

2. Read Proverbs 26:11 and Luke 15:15-16. Discuss the meaning of "dogs and swine" as they relate to "gifts and pearls."

3. Are there ever any situations where a believer should walk away from sharing the good news of the Gospel? (See Matthew 10:14; Acts 13:44-51; 18:5-6; and 28:17-28.)

Chapter 19
NEVER GONNA GIVE YOU UP
The Life that Never Quits

"Ask, and it will be given to you; seek, and you will find; knock, and it will be opened to you. For everyone who asks receives, and he who seeks finds, and to him who knocks it will be opened."

—Matthew 7:7-8

I had a friend who took a class in college taught by a rather humorous professor. He told me that, at the very beginning of the course, the professor made a declaration as to his style of teaching.

"Class, when I am teaching, if I happen to say something twice (or more), that means it is important and is probably going to be on the next test. If you do not pay attention, write it down, and study it, you are going to find yourself out of luck come test time."

Sure enough, over the course of the semester, the professor would be lecturing and would be making a point: "So, we find that in this equation, X divided by Y equals Z. X divided by Y equals Z. Oh, look—I said that two times. What does that mean?"

"That it's going to be on the test!" the class responded in unison.

"That's right! And what happens if you don't study that and remember it?" the professor inquired.

THE SERMON

"We are outta luck!" came the response.

Here in Matthew 7, our Lord returns to the importance of prayer for the third time. So far, we have been instructed on where to pray (in secret), and what to pray (the model prayer). Now, we come to the subject of how to pray.

One of the common marks found throughout Jesus' teaching on prayer is the brevity and simplicity of His prayers. In the Uncommon Life, prayer is the very breath that sustains the soul. It is the method of communication that reaches beyond our immediate surroundings and into a place of intimacy with God. It doesn't rely on theological platitudes, empty rhetoric, or an Ivy League vocabulary. Prayer is a conversation; prayer is a lifeline. Prayer is getting honest with the God of the universe about our struggles, needs, thoughts, desires, concerns, and failings. Prayer is not limited to circumstances, present realities, or political correctness. Prayer is being consistent in our beliefs in spite of reality, and persistent in our call in the face of impossibility.

Before we look at the *how* of prayer, let's review and reveal the hindrances to effective prayer. What are those things that hold us back from entering into the presence of God in the life of prayer?

HINDERING ATTITUDES IN PRAYER

1. *Do not pray unnaturally.*

> *"And when you pray, you shall not be like the hypocrites. For they love to pray standing in the synagogues and on the corners of the streets, that they may be seen by men. Assuredly, I say to you, they have their reward. But you, when you pray, go into your room, and when you have shut your door, pray to your Father who is in the secret place; and your Father who sees in secret will reward you openly. And when you pray, do*

not use vain repetitions as the heathen do. For they think that they will be heard for their many words" (Matthew 6:5-7).

The word *unnatural* can have many connotations in the context of prayer. First, it can refer to *where* we pray. Prayer is more a private experience than a public exercise. Some people think they sound more spiritual if, when praying in public, they pray long and lofty prayers in King James English. While this may sound impressive to some, Jesus was a first-century Jew, not a 17th-century Englishman, and religious exhibitionism is an affront to God.

The fact is that we can pray in our own private place. We can pray everywhere and at all times ("pray without ceasing"). All of this can be done without an audience, a stage, or a soapbox.

Second, the *how* of prayer is important. The power of prayer is not related to volume. God is not hard of hearing, and does not need you to scream at Him in order to be heard. Passion in prayer is fine as long as it is accompanied by the right motivation.

I once heard the story of a young pastor who was leading in prayer at his new church. In the course of his prayer, he got louder and louder. Finally, an elder spoke up, saying, "Pastor, God is not deaf!"

"I know," came the pastor's reply. "But He's a long way from *this* church."

Third, be careful of the unnatural prayer that is simply relaying information or teaching. Prayer should not be used as an information time or gossip session. A person who is asked to pray should not use that time as a way of lecturing others with their "vast wisdom and knowledge." God, as Creator of the universe, does not need us to inform Him of the goings-on in our lives, nor does He need us to attempt to manipulate others through guilt or sympathy. It is the Holy Spirit's job to convict people's hearts.

THE SERMON

God is aware of our circumstances before the thoughts enter our minds. Prayer does not have to be loud, lengthy, or lofty to garner God's attention. Prayer is a conversation with our heavenly Father. Nothing should be more natural.

2. *Do not pray unrepentantly.* Note these two warnings from Scripture:

- *"But your iniquities have separated you from your God; and your sins have hidden His face from you, so that He will not hear"* (Isaiah 59:2).

- *"If I regard iniquity in my heart, the Lord will not hear"* (Psalm 66:18).

When we hold on to strongholds, secret sins, and stubborn unrepentance, we are separated from the intimacy and fellowship we could enjoy with our heavenly Father.

3. *Do not pray with the wrong motivation.* God sees our heart and knows why we ask for what we ask for in prayer. The Apostle James said, *"You ask and do not receive, because you ask amiss, that you may spend it on your pleasures"* (James 4:3).

4. *Do not pray with an unforgiving spirit.* Jesus said, *"Whenever you stand praying, if you have anything against anyone, forgive him, that your Father in heaven may also forgive you your trespasses. But if you do not forgive, neither will your Father in heaven forgive your trespasses"* (Mark 11:25-26).

Jesus spells out the consequences of unforgiveness in no uncertain terms. Failure to forgive another person invites judgment from God, plain and simple.

5. *Do not pray with an ungenerous spirit.* Proverbs 21:13

says, *"Whoever shuts his ears to the cry of the poor will also cry himself and not be heard."*

Throughout Scripture, God places a great deal of value on how we treat the poor (especially orphans and widows). To ignore the needs of others is to invite isolation and a deaf ear in our time of need.

6. *Do not pray with an undisciplined home.* Before we can pray effectively, we must make sure our lives are in order; that goes for our home life as well.

> *Wives, likewise, be submissive to your own husbands, that even if some do not obey the word, they, without a word, may be won by the conduct of their wives, when they observe your chaste conduct accompanied by fear. Do not let your adornment be merely outward—arranging the hair, wearing gold, or putting on fine apparel—rather let it be the hidden person of the heart, with the incorruptible beauty of a gentle and quiet spirit, which is very precious in the sight of God. For in this manner, in former times, the holy women who trusted in God also adorned themselves, being submissive to their own husbands, as Sarah obeyed Abraham, calling him lord, whose daughters you are if you do good and are not afraid with any terror.*
>
> *Husbands, likewise, dwell with them with understanding, giving honor to the wife, as to the weaker vessel, and as being heirs together of the grace of life, that your prayers may not be hindered* (1 Peter 3:1-7).

THE SERMON

HELPFUL ACTIONS IN PRAYER

1. *Ask for what you need.*

When we are commanded to "ask," it implies there is Someone who can answer your need or request. There is Someone bigger than your problem, who is available for your entreating. In Jeremiah 33:3, we have this promise: *"Call to Me, and I will answer you, and show you great and mighty things, which you do not know."*

2. *Seek for what you have lost.*

Now we begin to see a progression of intensity. How many of us have lost something we had to have? Car keys? A birth certificate? A tax return from five years ago? The recipe your grandmother gave you for her oatmeal-walnut cookies? When we lose something important to us—something we need to function (like cookies)—we take action to find it.

The same was true in Jesus' day:

> *"What man of you, having a hundred sheep, if he loses one of them, does not leave the ninety-nine in the wilderness, and go after the one which is lost until he finds it?"* (Luke 15:4).

> *"Or what woman, having ten silver coins, if she loses one coin, does not light a lamp, sweep the house, and search carefully until she finds it? And when she has found it, she calls her friends and neighbors together, saying, 'Rejoice with me, for I have found the piece which I lost!'"* (Luke 15:8-9).

There are those times we ask, pouring our desires and needs out to God, and He seems to respond with silence. We ask and plead, but it seems He is distant, and our prayers seem to be getting no higher than the ceiling. Maybe that was how the children of Israel were

238

feeling when God spoke to them through Jeremiah: *"You will seek Me and find Me, when you search for Me with all your heart"* (Jeremiah 29:13).

There comes a moment when just asking isn't enough. What have you lost? What has the enemy stolen? Seeking God's face with all that is within us brings with it the promise that we will find; God will bring back what we thought was lost. The reason I say "thought" is that, in seeking Him with all of our hearts and getting into proper alignment with His goals and priorities, sometimes we find that what we thought we lost or needed is no longer important. We find that in seeking Him, we discover all we truly need.

"For thus says the Lord to the house of Israel: 'Seek Me and live'" (Amos 5:4).

3. ***Knock*** *for what you have been shut out of.*

There are some doors that will simply not open for you without the Lord's favor. They are things from which you are shut out—comfort, knowledge, hope, opportunity, favor, blessing, intimacy with God, and for some, Heaven itself. It starts off with this premise and promise from Jesus: *"All that the Father gives Me will come to Me, and the one who comes to Me I will by no means cast out"* (John 6:37).

A door implies an opening to another area or level. Doors are designed to shut out; to keep undesirable things and people out of a given space. Doors are also designed to be a point of welcome and security. When a groom carries his bride through the doorway, he is carrying her to a place of peace, security, and intimacy.

When we come to a door that is shut, we must knock in order to get the attention of the person inside who can open the door. And while God sees and knows everything, our exercise of knocking is a

THE SERMON

sign of obedience and faith. We knock in faith believing there is a God who can open every shut door.

Notice that this door has a promise: "It shall be opened." You may be discouraged, but keep on knocking. You may be tired, but keep on knocking. Others may ridicule, but keep on knocking. Your spiritual "knuckles" might be bruised and bleeding, but keep on knocking.

So, child of God, Jesus repeated all of that about prayer. Do you think it might just be important? Do you think it might be on the test?

Let's look at that progression one more time:

- Ask . . . dependence . . . Father

- Seek . . . persistence . . . Holy Spirit

- Knock . . . insistence . . . Jesus

"These things says He who is holy, He who is true, 'He who has the key of David, He who opens and no one shuts, and shuts and no one opens'" (Revelation 3:7).

Any door that God opens, no one will be able to shut.

Many years ago, a famous lawsuit developed when the Mississippi steamboat community got an injunction to prevent the railroad from building a bridge across the Mississippi River. A famous orator of the day, a man named Judge Wead, spoke for two hours on behalf of the river people. When he sat down, those gathered erupted into applause and cheers.

When the crowd calmed down, the lawyer for the railroad spoke. While Judge Wead had spoken for an extended period, this awkward country lawyer delivered his argument in about one minute.

"First, I want to congratulate my opponent upon his wonderful oration," the lawyer complimented his rival. "I never heard a finer speech. But it had nothing to do with the main issue. The only question for you to decide, gentlemen of the jury, is whether a man has more right to travel up and down the river than he has to cross the river."

With that, the tall, gawky lawyer sat down. It didn't take the jury long to decide in favor of the railroad, and its short-spoken country lawyer.

And who was the lawyer for the railroad, you ask?

Abraham Lincoln. [61]

"A word fitly spoken is like apples of gold in settings of silver" (Proverbs 25:11).

Three times now; you got it?

Prayer—the *how* is as important as the *what*. Pray with the trajectory of His will, with the passion of His purpose, with the persistence and confidence in His promises, and with the simplicity and intimacy of a child sitting in His lap.

The good news is that you're not "outta luck." Quite the opposite— you are blessed beyond measure.

Class dismissed.

THE SERMON

KEY QUESTIONS TO PONDER
Chapter 19: *Never Gonna Give You Up*

1. Three times Jesus teaches the importance of prayer.

He taught us:

_____ to pray (Matthew 6:6).

_____ to pray (6:9-13).

_____ to pray (7:7-8).

Discuss each.

2. Read Jeremiah 29:13 and Amos 5:4. Jesus used three words to describe the intensity of prayer: *Ask*, *seek*, and *knock*. Are these three words a progression, or do they all convey the same meaning?

3. Discuss the following parables: Luke 11:5-10 and 18:1-6. What lessons can you learn from these?

What do they have in common?

Chapter 20
IT'S A CELEBRATION
The Life Lived as a Son

"Or what man is there among you who, if his son asks for bread, will give him a stone? Or if he asks for a fish, will he give him a serpent? If you then, being evil, know how to give good gifts to your children, how much more will your Father who is in heaven give good things to those who ask Him!"

—Matthew 7:9-11 (NIV)

God hears and answers the one who asks, seeks, and knocks. Jesus leaves no question that the Father has our best interests at heart, and is not going to pull a bait-and-switch when it comes to giving good gifts to His children. But how exactly does this happen? How does God answer the passionate seeker?

He Answers as a Loving Father.

God desires to be our Father, and views those who belong to Him as His children. How does God become our Father? After all, there are those who believe we are all God's children. The problem with this "theology" is that it does not line up with Scripture. On the contrary, the Bible declares that those who are not followers of Jesus Christ are *"of their father, the devil"* (John 8:44).

THE SERMON

Regardless of what pop culture, feel-good motivational speakers, and song lyrics devoid of Scriptural content preach, the Bible makes a sharp distinction between "children of God" and "children of wrath" (and "sons of disobedience").

Ephesians 2:2-3 puts it this way: *"In which you once walked according to the course of this world, according to the prince of the power of the air, the spirit who now works in the sons of disobedience, among whom also we all once conducted ourselves in the lusts of our flesh, fulfilling the desires of the flesh and of the mind, and were by nature children of wrath, just as the others."*

In my mind, this Scripture passage conjures images of the Dickens-esque orphans and street urchins depicted in stories like *Oliver Twist*: dirty-faced and tattered-clothes delinquents, scraping, fighting, and thieving their way through life on the desperate, dark, and dirty streets of 19th century London, without the loving and guiding hand of a father. While they may have had a flawed father-figure in their lives, they don't know a Father with the power to deliver them from the poverty and squalor of their existence—a Father with the power to give them a new life. The Scriptures declare that all people must be "born again." There is only one Father with the power to make that happen: Jehovah God.

John reiterated this in his Gospel when he quoted the words of Jesus: *"Most assuredly, I say to you, unless one is born again, he cannot see the kingdom of God"* (3:3).

But being born again does not just end with a simple act, and that's it. The act of being born again (accepting Christ as Savior) is the first act or step in a Spirit-filled life and lifestyle. *"For as many as are led by the Spirit of God, these are sons of God. For you did not receive the spirit of bondage again to fear, but you received the Spirit of adoption by whom we cry out, 'Abba, Father.' The Spirit Himself bears witness with our spirit that we are children of God, and if children, then heirs—heirs of God and joint heirs with Christ, if indeed we suffer with Him, that we may also be glorified together"* (Romans 8:14-17).

"And because you are sons, God has sent forth the Spirit of His Son into your hearts, crying out, 'Abba, Father!' Therefore you are no longer a slave but a son, and if a son, then an heir of God through Christ" (Galatians 4:6-7).

We've all heard the saying "Children should be seen, not heard." We've all seen the parents who treat their children more as slaves than as sons and daughters. In these two passages, Paul makes it clear that our relationship to God is not as a servant or slave, but as children who can cry out to our Father, and that all of the resources of His Kingdom are at our disposal. His Word is filled with hope, promise, and assurance that God is our everlasting Father.

He Answers as a Knowing Father.

"Or what man is there among you who, if his son asks for bread, will give him a stone? Or if he asks for a fish, will he give him a serpent?" (Matthew 7:9-10).

While this passage speaks to the fact that the onus is on us to ask, it further reiterates that God's gifts are appropriate, and will not hurt us. Jesus is making a contrast that the people listening to Him on the mount that day could understand. If He were speaking to a crowd in the 21st century, He might say, "What man listening to me today would give his son a rock if he asked for a sandwich, or a live rattlesnake if he asked for grilled salmon?"

It is, however, important to note that "yes" is not the only answer to a question or request. Oftentimes, we think God is not hearing us

THE SERMON

because we are not seeing the response we hoped for to our petition. We often forget that "no" is just as valid a response as "yes." When we make a request, our limited sight may not reveal to us the pitfalls of what we are asking for. But God has 20/20 vision of everything in our path. Sometimes difficult answers and experiences come from His hand to discipline us and correct us. Sometimes the undesired answer for us is His way of protecting us. The bottom line is this: He knows our needs.

> *For consider Him who endured such hostility from sinners against Himself, lest you become weary and discouraged in your souls. You have not yet resisted to bloodshed, striving against sin. And you have forgotten the exhortation which speaks to you as to sons: "My son, do not despise the chastening of the Lord, nor be discouraged when you are rebuked by Him; for whom the Lord loves He chastens, and scourges every son whom He receives."*

> *If you endure chastening, God deals with you as with sons; for what son is there whom a father does not chasten? But if you are without chastening, of which all have become partakers, then you are illegitimate and not sons. Furthermore, we have had human fathers who corrected us, and we paid them respect. Shall we not much more readily be in subjection to the Father of spirits and live? For they indeed for a few days chastened us as seemed best to them, but He for our profit, that we may be partakers of His holiness. Now no chastening seems to be joyful for the present, but painful; nevertheless, afterward it yields the peaceable fruit of righteousness to those who have been trained by it* (Hebrews 12:3-11).

Chastening and discipline take a variety of forms and are never pleasant. Yet any chastening that comes from the Father should be considered a good sign, because God makes it clear in this passage that He chastens His own. If God is disciplining you in some way, that is a sign that you are His, and He is doing it out of love for His child. His discipline trains us and molds us into the image of Jesus.

During the time of Christ, most vessels were made out of pottery. The process of making a pottery vessel requires time and patience. The clay has to be dug out of the ground. It has to be worked and formed into the desired shape. Oftentimes, it is a process of trial and error before the proper form is attained. Once the clay is formed, it must be fired in a kiln in order to harden and be usable. In several passages (such as 2 Timothy 2:21), the Bible refers to us as "vessels." In order for us to be usable, we must go through the fires of chastening and discipline, according to the plan God has for each of us.

"Therefore humble yourselves under the mighty hand of God, that He may exalt you in due time, casting all your care upon Him, for He cares for you" (1 Peter 5:6-7).

He Answers as a Giving Father.

"If you then, being evil, know how to give good gifts to your children, how much more will your Father who is in heaven give good things to those who ask Him!" (Matthew 7:11).

The best of earthly fathers is a poor imitation of our heavenly Father. We are born into sin, but for all of our failings, I think it would be safe to say that most fathers, regardless of socio-economic class, desire to give good things to their children. We may not even know exactly what that is, but we try, nonetheless. God gives to His children only those things that are good for us. He knows what is best. The

THE SERMON

things that flow from His hand and His abundance are always meant for our good.

In Luke 11:13, Jesus said, *"If you then, being evil, know how to give good gifts to your children, how much more will your heavenly Father give the Holy Spirit to those who ask Him!"*

"How much more." Regardless of all the good we give to our children, God will give exceedingly more of the Holy Spirit to those of us, His children, who ask Him. His gifts are conveyed to us by His primary gift—the Holy Spirit. God is not looking for us to be satisfied with living the "just-enough" life. He has made available the "much more" life, and it is ours for the asking! And that is not just wishful thinking. The "how much more" life is a promise. The Holy Spirit is God's promised gift to all who are His, to all who will ask. Jesus said, *"Behold, I send the Promise of My Father upon you; but tarry in the city of Jerusalem until you are endued with power from on high"* (Luke 24:49).

The presence of the Holy Spirit in our life of is the conduit by which we receive His gifts. There is some debate on the actual number of gifts of the Spirit. Depending on who is counting, there are 18 or 19 gifts of the Spirit listed in Scripture. These gifts are ours as a down payment of the glory to come, and allow us to operate, in this life, in His supernatural power and anointing.

Beyond the gifts of the Spirit, the presence of the Holy Spirit in our life verifies that we are, in fact, children of God: *"For as many as are led by the Spirit of God, these are sons of God"* (Romans 8:14).

The Holy Spirit gives us direction in our daily lives, and by virtue of that leading, we can have confidence that we are the sons and daughters of the Most High.

He's the Father of Supply.

Peter came a long way from the over-eager, quick-tempered, and weak-kneed disciple we see sitting at the feet of Jesus while the Master delivered the words of these passages in Matthew. Jesus referred to him as "the rock" in Matthew 16, and true to Christ's words, Peter indeed became a rock of the early Church. By the time he wrote his letters to the believers throughout Asia Minor, we see a maturity brought about by years of not only serving alongside the Master, but serving His people through selflessness and sacrifice.

Peter understood not just what it took to live the Uncommon Life, but also the qualities and process it takes to recognize and realize the supply of God in our lives. Just like ascending a staircase step-by-step, Peter recognized the process. He understood that the key to accessing the supply of God is following the process, and trusting the God of the process. He wrote in 2 Peter 1:5-7:

- *Add to faith, virtue*

- *To virtue, knowledge*

- *To knowledge, self-control*

- *To self-control, perseverance*

- *To perseverance, godliness*

- *To godliness, brotherly kindness*

- *To brotherly kindness, love.*

Peter added that not following the process is *shortsighted* and *blind*, and shows the individual *"has forgotten that he was cleansed from his old sins"* (vv. 8-9).

So how about you? Are you shortsighted, or a recipient of all

THE SERMON

things? Are you blind and forgetful of the grace by which you stand, or are you a partaker of the divine nature? Will you take hold of the great and precious promises and be fruitful and successful in your calling, or will retreat to the emptiness and ignorance of a barren, unfruitful, and common life?

Heaven is waiting for God's children to walk on the sure footing of our divine call, and to live and operate in the knowledge of our Lord Jesus Christ. Our abundant entrance to the kingdom is waiting—the key to the gate is the Uncommon Life!

KEY QUESTIONS TO PONDER
Chapter 20: *It's a Celebration*

1. Read Romans 8:14-17 and Galatians 4:6-7. With these two passages as a backdrop, discuss the difference between a "slave" and a "son."

2. Read Luke 11:11-13. Do you agree or disagree with the following statement? *God's gifts are conveyed to us by His primary gift of the Holy Spirit. He isn't looking for us to be satisfied with living the "just enough" life He has made available the "much more" life, and it is ours for the asking.* Explain your answer.

3. Are you walking in all the great and precious promises described in 2 Peter 1:2-11? If not, why not?

Chapter 21
THE SECRET OF SUCCESS
The Life That Is Well-Lived

"So in everything, do to others what you would have them do to you, for this sums up the Law and the Prophets"

—Matthew 7:12 (NIV)

This verse, often called the Golden Rule, is one of the best-known sayings in history. It is "the essence of all that is taught" (NLT) in the Scriptures regarding relationships.

Years ago, when I taught in seminary, I asked a group of students, "What is the Golden Rule?" A quick response came from the back of the room: "He who has the gold makes the rules!"

We all laughed at this remark, but amidst the laughter, I felt a twinge of sadness. This remark has its roots in the business community where this attitude is, in many cases, a reality.

In the financial collapse of 2008, many ordinary people lost much of their savings and retirement, while executives at the top of failing companies took multi-million dollar bonuses. This kind of greed flies in the face of not just decent society, but Scripture itself.

A well-lived life means more than making money and being successful personally. It is characterized by a life lived selflessly for

THE SERMON

others. Based on that criteria, one could say Mother Teresa was far more successful than someone like an oil magnate or a media tycoon. A life lived according to the Golden Rule places great emphasis on our treatment of others.

What exactly is the Golden Rule?

THE GOLDEN RULE'S CONTEXT

Jesus is concluding the Sermon on the Mount, and is wrapping up this last segment on judging others. Obviously, no one wants to be judged, especially not harshly or hypocritically. Furthermore, no one sets out to squander their deposit of truth on someone who would only turn on them or stab them in the back.

If you are like me, as you look back on this great sermon, you come to realize not just how you want to be treated, but how to treat others as well. What we expect for ourselves, we should always be willing to make available to those around us, as much as is within our power. We must confess our needs to the Father, but always with the expectation that we will offer what we receive to others:

- Mercy

- Forgiveness

- Prayer

- Sanctity of marriage

- Desire to obey the Law

- Spiritual Discipline

- Discernment.

Some years ago, a friend of mine was asked to speak at a men's conference, and share a bit of his testimony. His story included a time he was away from the Lord, and had entered into an affair with a married woman. He was also married with children. In spite of his infidelity, his wife chose to stay with him. God healed their marriage and their family, and at this conference, he had the opportunity to share about forgiveness, restoration, and hope.

When the conference ended on Sunday morning, he was greeted face-to-face by a man who had, in years past, done great harm to his family. My friend realized if he was going to practice what he had just preached, he had no choice but to forgive. He told me, "I was never that anxious to forgive, particularly that individual, until I became the one in need of forgiveness. When I saw his face, I understood that."

Whether it is mercy, grace, forgiveness, or hope, we must always be willing to pass on those "good and perfect gifts" we receive from the Father to those we come into contact with.

THE GOLDEN RULE'S CONTENT

Over the centuries, people have consulted sages, rabbis, teachers, and leaders for direction on how they should treat others. In this passage, Jesus instructs us not to consult an outside voice or opinion, but our own soul. Exactly how should we treat those around us? For the answer to that question, we need only ask ourselves in every situation, "How do I want someone to respond to me?"

Our heavenly Father gives us His example, in that He responds to His children lovingly, mercifully, honestly, and generously. In responding to others by following His example, we are exhibiting Christlikeness, modeling the words spoken Paul to the Galatians 2:20: *"I have been crucified with Christ; it is no longer I who live, but Christ*

THE SERMON

lives in me; and the life which I now live in the flesh I live by faith in the Son of God, who loved me and gave Himself for me."

How we treat others should always be a reflection of how we desire to be treated. How we treat others will determine our own future. At the end of Matthew 7:12, Jesus declared, *"This sums up the Law and the Prophets."* We could easily translate that into our modern vernacular by saying, "This is what the Bible is all about." This is why God gave us the Law. This is why we see example after example, from Genesis to Revelation, of how to treat and not treat others. From the conflict of Cain and Abel, to the friendship of David and Jonathan, to the way Jesus interacted with His disciples, and how His disciples interacted with each other, we see positive and negative examples of how to live with others. The lesson that comes to the surface is that the Law was given so we could live in a decent society. The Law was given so we would understand how to treat others. Subsequently, this is why we have the prophetic word, so we can release into others what they need for the future.

The power of the spoken word is often undervalued in our society. No one can put a price on the value of a compliment, a word of encouragement, or well-spoken godly advice. The tongue is a valuable instrument just as it is a lethal weapon. How many individuals sit in prisons today because of the lack of positive reinforcement, be it word or deed, from an authority figure? How many reading this book have given up on a dream because of belittling words spoken by someone close? At the same time, how many have gone on to greatness because of a timely word or encouragement from an unexpected place? We all want great things for ourselves and those close to us. This verse makes it clear that what we desire for ourselves should be reflected in how we treat those we come into contact with.

THE GOLDEN RULE'S CONCEPT

Here is the principle of generosity applied to relationships, not money. In today's society, whenever we hear someone talk about being generous, our minds instantly turn to financial gain. However, the Uncommon Life measures things like success and generosity in much more than financial terms. Actually, the most ancient principle for success in Scripture is the principle of seed-time and harvest.

First, we need to look back to Genesis 3, where man blew it. The earth is judged, and man now has to live in an environment of hostility and difficulty. The very ground was cursed as a result of the Fall. The Lord told Adam: *"Cursed is the ground for your sake; in toil you shall eat of it all the days of your life. Both thorns and thistles it shall bring forth for you, and you shall eat the herb of the field. In the sweat of your face you shall eat bread till you return to the ground, for out of it you were taken; for dust you are, and to dust you shall return"* (Genesis 3:17-19).

After the Flood, however, God set forth a principle and promise for blessing, which is the principle of sowing and reaping. He promised Noah, *"I will never again curse the ground for man's sake. . . . While the earth remains, seedtime and harvest . . . shall not cease"* (Genesis 8:20-22).

Yet, the process of sowing and reaping is difficult, as any farmer can tell you. Breaking up tough ground, sowing seed, keeping the ground weeded and watered—it all takes time and diligence. But God is just, in both His judgment and His mercy. While the process of sowing and reaping may take time and effort, the reward is a bountiful harvest. The Apostle Paul wrote, *"He who sows sparingly will also reap sparingly, and he who sows bountifully will also reap bountifully"* (2 Corinthians 9:6).

THE SERMON

God is not a cruel God who, because of the failure of Adam and Eve (and everyone since then), was going to just hang us out to dry. He offers us a path to repentance and prosperity if we are willing to accept it. Again, that path pertains not just to the physical and tangible world around us (food, drink, resources, etc.), but to the less tangible qualities of life as well. In this verse, Paul instructs us to sow into the lives of others what we need ourselves. However, there is wisdom involved in sowing and reaping. There are immutable laws of nature (set up by God at creation) that don't change simply because we wish it or have good intentions. There are principles involved in farming that will determine the success or failure of one's crop:

- You don't sow corn in the middle of winter.
- You don't sow tomatoes with the expectation of reaping cucumbers.
- You wouldn't sow seed in the middle of a flood.
- You don't expect to begin harvesting three days after you plant the seed.
- You don't scatter seed on a concrete parking lot.

Any one of these things is a recipe for failure. It matters *when* you sow, *what* you sow, *how* you sow, and *where* you sow. It requires you to wait, sometimes longer than others, depending on the type of seed. But the law of sowing and reaping also assumes more than a 1:1 ratio. Think about the number of ears of corn that come from a single stalk, or how many apples come from a tree that was birthed from a single seed.

With that understanding, the spiritual principle at play is clear:

- Need forgiveness? Then forgive.
- Need mercy? Offer mercy.

THE SECRET OF MY SUCCESS

- Need help? Assist those in need.

- Need money? Give to those who need financial help.

- Need more time? Give some time to others.

- Need love? Give love to those around you.

Another principle of seedtime and harvest I heard articulated by Jentezen Franklin is this:

Seed . . . T . . . I . . . M . . . E . . . and Harvest.

Just as in the physical realm, things sown in the spiritual dimension— less tangible things like forgiveness, mercy, love, etc.—also take time to germinate, bloom, and become obvious. While I have seen things such as forgiveness and mercy happen almost immediately, they usually don't happen overnight. The Golden Rule is simply this: We will receive what we give in relationships. It may not always happen in the time frame we wish for, or from the source or manner in which we expect, but God keeps His promises. Living the Uncommon Life means learning to recognize His goodness in whatever form it takes.

You may say, "That sounds too simple, too cut-and-dry. How am I supposed to live and respond when I sow into someone and I get nothing in return? What do I do when my goodwill is not reciprocated?"

You're right. It's not always cut-and-dry. But if you remember back a few chapters in this book, Jesus covered that. He said those who are persecuted for His sake will be rewarded (Matthew 5:11-12). Later He said we must not seek revenge, but instead we should love our enemies (vv. 38-46).

Looking back at the beginning of this chapter, do you remember how Matthew 7:12 begins? *"So in everything . . ."*

THE SERMON

Those three words signify there are no limits on this call to Spirit-filled living; no caveats with the Uncommon Life. That means regardless of our circumstances, regardless of how we feel, regardless of what happened when we got out of bed, on our way to work, at the store, or at church, we have an expectation from God to live in accordance with the Golden Rule. Heavy? Yes. Full of blessing and promise? Again, yes.

In the Greek text, this whole verse is present tense, meaning continuous action. The phrase about treating others is an imperative—a continuous command. Jesus is telling us, "In every situation, go on doing to others what you want them to do for you."

THE POWER OF FORGIVENESS

When Dana was 16 years old, his father was tragically killed in an automobile accident on the way to church one Sunday evening. He tells the story below.

> *My dad was the assistant pastor at the church we attended. On a sunny Sunday night in June, he and my mom and I were on our way to church when a sports car crossed the center line of the road we were on. It hit our station wagon nearly head-on and, with a combined velocity of about 90 miles per hour, killed my dad almost instantly. My mom and I were not expected to live through the night. The woman who hit us, as well as her husband who was riding with her, both walked away from the accident, almost unscathed. We survived, and over the course of the next months, we found some physical healing and restoration. Still, the biggest hole was the emotional one left by the absence of my father.*
>
> *In the aftermath of the accident came the criminal trial. The woman who hit us was charged with, among other*

THE SECRET OF MY SUCCESS

things, driving under the influence. Blood tests revealed she had taken a cocktail of depressant drugs, both legal and illegal. Over a year after the accident, *I found myself sitting in a courtroom, looking into the face of the person who had robbed me of my dad. After nearly a week of judicial proceedings, the jury found the woman guilty of second-degree murder, carrying a minimum sentence of ten years in prison. She was immediately sent off to jail to await her transfer to prison.*

Two months later, we received word that the judge, through a judicial maneuver, had overruled the jury, reducing her charge and her sentence, and releasing her from prison. After more legal proceedings, a higher court ruled with the district attorney that the judge was "out of line," that she was guilty, and he had to sentence her. The judge promptly sentenced her to ten years, then suspended the sentence in the next breath.

My father was gone, my family was devastated, and the person responsible only served two months for it. How was this justice?

A few months later, I found myself walking through our local mall. I was on a lunch break from work, and having eaten, I was leaving the mall. As I approached the exit, I heard someone call my name from above me. It was a friend of mine who, unknown to me, was working maintenance at the mall. He was on a ladder above me, and called out to me. As we stood talking, I happened to glance across the mall, and realized where I was standing—right in front of the business owned by the father of the young woman whom had killed my father. I noticed this man, whom I had seen in the courtroom

261

THE SERMON

during the trial, was standing in the doorway looking my direction. I turned back to my friend and continued our discussion. A few seconds later, I heard a voice behind me say my name. I turned around to find myself face-to-face with "her" father.

"Dana, if you would, I'd like you to come in and meet my daughter," came his humble request.

Every natural instinct within me—every bone in my body—wanted to turn and walk the other direction, wanting nothing to do with this man or his daughter. Yet, something inside of me wouldn't allow me to turn. Something inside of me realized, at that moment, what mercy and grace had been shown to me, and my opportunity to offer the same. Something inside of me knew that to retreat from this opportunity to face the person responsible for my father's death would keep me bound to the feelings of anger and pain I had felt for the past nearly two years.

As I followed this man into his shop, and looked into the face of the person who had caused me such immeasurable pain, the anger and pain gave way to forgiveness and grace—the same forgiveness and grace I needed every day before and since. The same forgiveness and grace that I understood a little bit better after that day.

Corrie ten Boom once said, when describing those who had suffered at the hands of the Nazis during World War II: "Those who were able to forgive their former enemies were able also to return to the outside world and rebuild their lives, no matter what the physical scars. Those who nursed their bitterness remained invalids. It was as simple and as horrible as that."[62]

THE SECRET OF MY SUCCESS

So, what is the secret of your success?

Jesus summed up the entire 39 books of the Old Testament with this verse in Matthew. What's more, we find this verse at the heart of the New Covenant—the Gospel.

What is the result? Think back to the beginning of the Sermon on the Mount. Nine times He promises "blessings," and all of the requirements for those blessings we find summed up in the Golden Rule. What are those promises we find back in Matthew 5?

Heaven (v. 3)

Comfort (v. 4)

Earthly inheritance and blessing (v. 5)

Spiritual fullness and righteousness (v. 6)

Mercy (v. 7)

Visions of God (v. 8)

Sonship (v. 9)

Kingdom inheritance (v. 10)

Eternal Kingdom reward (v. 11-12)

The Golden Rule offers admission to the illuminated path to peace, contentment, and freedom. The Golden Rule is the key to the passageway to the Uncommon Life.

THE SERMON

KEY QUESTIONS TO PONDER

Chapter 21: *The Secret of My Success*

1. What is the "Golden Rule"?

2. All the promises and requirements of "happy living" as outlined in the Sermon on the Mount are summed up in the Golden Rule. Go back to Matthew 5 and list all those promises.

3. Is there a difference between *mercy* and *grace*? If so, explain.

Chapter 22
YOU HAVE CHOSEN _____
The Life that Journeys the Road Less Travelled

"Enter by the narrow gate; for wide is the gate and broad is the way that leads to destruction, and there are many who go in by it. Because narrow is the gate and difficult is the way which leads to life, and there are few who find it.

Beware of false prophets, who come to you in sheep's clothing, but inwardly they are ravenous wolves. You will know them by their fruits. Do men gather grapes from thorn bushes or figs from thistles? Even so, every good tree bears good fruit, but a bad tree bears bad fruit. A good tree cannot bear bad fruit, nor can a bad tree bear good fruit. Every tree that does not bear good fruit is cut down and thrown into the fire. Therefore by their fruits you will know them.

Not everyone who says to Me, 'Lord, Lord,' shall enter the kingdom of heaven, but he who does the will of My Father in heaven. Many will say to Me in that day, 'Lord, Lord, have we not prophesied in Your name, cast out demons in Your name, and done many wonders in Your name?' And then I will declare to them, 'I never knew you; depart from Me, you who practice lawlessness!'"

—Matthew 7:13-23

THE SERMON

In the blockbuster film *Indiana Jones and the Last Crusade*, when Indiana Jones and his nemesis Walter Donovan reach the hidden chamber which has housed the Holy Grail (the legendary cup of Christ from the Last Supper) for centuries, they come face-to-face with the ancient knight who has guarded the grail since the time of the Crusades. The old knight issues them a challenge—they most chose the grail from among the dozens of cups in the chamber. To choose the right cup would mean eternal life, and to choose the wrong would mean certain death.

When the evil Donovan proceeds to choose, he looks at all of the ornate and beautiful glassware, choosing a beautifully-crafted cup—a vessel fit for a king. In the deadly aftermath of his choice, the old knight looks at Jones and stoically declares, "He chose poorly."

When Indiana approaches the assortment of cups, he chooses not from among the dozens of meticulously crafted works of art; he looks for the ugly, mundane, ordinary cup—"the cup of a carpenter." When he chooses a most ordinary, tarnished cup from among the collection, the old knight looks at him with a slight grin and says, "You have chosen wisely." [63]

Life is a journey, and those who travel the path of the Uncommon Life watch the road signs, notice the pitfalls, recognize the potholes, and understand that a wide, six-lane highway may be attractive in its smooth pavement and capacity for lots of traffic to pass unhindered at a rapid pace; but it won't necessarily get you to your desired destination. You can travel up and down I-95 until your wheels fall off, but if you are trying to get to Flagstaff, Arizona, you're just wasting time; I-95 is the main artery between Maine and Florida. Those who live the Uncommon Life read the warning labels, choose and operate in the wisdom derived from the Instruction Book (the

Bible) as opposed to the expediency of those who see the easy path that seems self-explanatory, and are not afraid to travel the lonely road of righteousness. But while living the Uncommon Life is about living above our circumstances, we have to keep a careful watch with regard to three areas of danger.

1. THE DANGER OF A FALSE PATHWAY

"Wide is the gate and broad is the way that leads to destruction, and there are many who go in by it. Because narrow is the gate and difficult is the way which leads to life, and there are few who find it."

In Matthew 7:13-14, we have before us a warning concerning our lives and destinies.

There are two directions of life. One is described as the broad and easy way. The other is described as the narrow way. This passage makes it clear the consequences of following either path. This same concept is found in Psalm 1, where the way of the righteous and the way of the ungodly are contrasted.

This contrast has to do with morality. There is a path of least resistance that gives free rein to the flesh. It is the way of moral laxity. It is a way without the discipline of the Word of God. It is the philosophy of selfish pleasure-seeking that permeates our society today. Self-gratification becomes the motive for living. This broad way has plenty of room for every opinion, idea, philosophy, and practice. It is the permissive road. While it may start out as a harmless looking country road, it gradually graduates to a four-lane highway, then a six-lane interstate, and eventually a 12-lane thoroughfare—a straight shot to destruction itself. Watching from the shoulder of the highway, you'll notice most of society travelling on this road today.

THE SERMON

On the other hand, the narrow way is the hard way. In the Greek, this passage reads, *"Made narrow is the way."* God has determined that we walk the narrow road. The guardrails of that road are the Word of God and the lordship of Jesus Christ. It is the toll road that requires acceptance of the blood of Jesus Christ for the forgiveness of sin as payment to pass.

There are two doors. We're all familiar with cartoons and comedies (or real life) where someone tries to walk through a door while carrying something too big for the doorway. It just doesn't work, and sometimes the outcome is quite comical. In the spiritual realm of life, there are two doors: one is wide, and the other is narrow. One is easy to see, and one is hard to find. The wide door is easy to pass through, even when loaded down with the baggage of life. However, the entrance to the narrow door is positioned at the foot of a bloody cross, and passage through it requires that we leave all of our baggage there in order to pass through.

There are two destinies. One of the more popular bumper stickers of the 21st century is one that uses a variety of religious or ideological symbols to spell out the word *Coexist.* The different images used represent Christianity, Judaism, Islam, Wicca, and Eastern religious philosophy. The idea illustrated by this bumper sticker is that we should simply coexist because all of these "religions" are equal. The problem with this idea is that it flies in the face of the truth that the Bible teaches. There are not many paths of truth, as the bumper sticker would have you believe. Truth is not subjective; being sincere does not mean being saved, and not all roads lead to Heaven.

It all comes down to a choice between Heaven and Hell. Jesus said, *"I am the Way, the Truth, and the Life: no one comes to the Father except through Me"* (John 14:6). Either Jesus is exactly who

He said He is, and He is the *only* way; or He was a liar, and His words are of no value. Religions that say He was just a prophet or a good man contradict themselves. It is impossible to logically sit on the fence with regard to the personhood of Christ, for He spoke only in absolutes. Either He is the Son of God and the only way to Heaven, or He was a delusional crazy man, more worthy of our pity than our worship. It is a logical impossibility to have it both ways.

While the decision may be difficult for some, the options are clear and simple: The narrow way leads to life, and the broad way leads to destruction. There is no neutral ground. There is no middle road. Any who believe otherwise are in great peril, for they believe they are on way to Heaven when, in fact, they are flying blindly down the road that leads to destruction.

2. THE DANGER OF A FALSE PROPHET

"Beware of false prophets, who come to you in sheep's clothing."

In the 20th century, we were faced with the Nazi atrocities of the Second World War. The leader of the Nazi party was the notorious Adolph Hitler. In 1925, he wrote in his autobiography, *Mein Kampf*: "But the most brilliant propagandist technique will yield no success unless one fundamental principle is borne in mind constantly and with unflagging attention. It must confine itself to a few points and repeat them over and over." [64]

As the mouthpiece for the Third Reich, Joseph Goebbels was the public-relations face of this demonic ideology. Goebbels played out his master's philosophy in spades. The vitriol and venom Goebbels spewed out over the German airwaves, at the behest of Hitler, resulted in the brutal execution of over six million Jews throughout Europe,

THE SERMON

not to mention scores of others who opposed the Nazi war machine of the 1930s and 1940s.

In today's world, we are faced with an onslaught of false information (propaganda). Everywhere we turn, ideas that challenge our ideas of right and wrong are thrown at us in various ways; some are subtle, and some more overt. We live in a time in which there is no shortage of fake news or false prophets. Those who would attempt to deceive us are more numerous than ever before. According to a university study, there are more than 25,000 gurus claiming to be Christ in our world today. So how do we recognize voices of deception and destruction today?

Notice their presence. Jesus declared there would be false prophets. Speaking to the Ephesian elders in Acts 20:28-31, Paul warned, *"Savage wolves will come in among you, not sparing the flock."* In fact, throughout the New Testament, we are warned of the danger of being led astray by religious charlatans.

Notice their practice. They appear in sheep's clothing. In other words, they look like a Christian, appear to be saved, and the works they do may even be generous and good, and of benefit to those around them. The problem is that what they do doesn't square up with the Word of God. Honestly, at times I have been deceived myself. There are many who look good, sound good, and say what they know people are eager to hear. The problem is that they have strayed from Scripture and sound teaching. What happens when a preacher moves away from the Word of God? The crowd he carries with him becomes a cult built around his personality rather than the personhood of Jesus.

Notice their perversity. Inside they are savage wolves. They have come to tear and scatter God's flock. Many of God's sheep have been wounded and rendered useless in the Kingdom by giving heed to false doctrine. Because churches and faith-based organizations are unwilling to call the disagreeable for what it is, they have allowed demonically-influenced men and women to fill leadership positions in religious bodies today.

Notice their product. The acid test of a prophet is the fruit of his or her ministry. Is the ministry bringing forth sound fruit or bad fruit? Is it gathering fruit or firewood? Even when their teaching and fruit may initially seem sound, eventually, those operating outside of the authority of the Word of God and the power of the Holy Spirit will reveal their true motivation; and their fruit will prove itself toxic to those under their influence. Jesus said, *"A good tree cannot bear bad fruit, nor can a bad tree bear good fruit."*

3. THE DANGER OF A FALSE PROFESSION

"Not everyone who says to Me, 'Lord, Lord,' shall enter the kingdom of heaven."

With these words, Jesus moves from talking about a false teacher to a false convert. This is the person who makes the verbal confession and yet is lost. Make no mistake, however: a verbal confession is necessary for salvation. In Romans 10:9-13, Paul wrote: *"That if you confess with your mouth the Lord Jesus and believe in your heart that God has raised Him from the dead, you will be saved. For with the heart one believes unto righteousness, and with the mouth confession is made unto salvation. For the Scripture says, 'Whoever believes on Him will not be put to shame.' For there is no distinction between Jew and Greek, for the same Lord over all is rich to all who call upon Him. For 'whoever calls on the name of the Lord shall be saved.'"*

THE SERMON

Yet an outward, verbal profession is not enough. This particular teaching by Jesus is startling—*"Many will say to Me in that day, 'Lord, Lord.'"*

• *It was a sound confession:* "Jesus is Lord." That is the essential confession of Christianity.

• *It was a fervent confession.* Twice, the people making the profession said, "Lord!" There was seemingly nothing dead about this confession. It was fervent and impassioned.

• *It was a public confession.* They had openly and publicly confessed Jesus to be Lord.

• *It was a powerful confession.* In the name of the Lord, they had spoken, cast out demons, and performed miracles. Yet, they are lost without Jesus.

• *It was a false confession.* It was a false confession because it was only verbal, not moral. Jesus once asked His disciples, *"But why do you call me 'Lord, Lord,' and not do the things which I say?"* (Luke 6:46).

It is possible to speak the truth about Jesus and even see results, yet not know Christ yourself. Balaam spoke the truth, but went to Hell (see 2 Peter 2:15).

How else do we explain the unfaithful who remain on our church rolls? How else do we explain the spiritual poverty of so many? How else do we explain the low moral life of so many professing Christians?

The answer is a *false* profession! A verbal profession that was correctly done, but led to no moral or spiritual change.

How tragic to hear the cry of this religious person on Judgment Day, followed by Jesus' reply: *"I never knew you."* Jesus does not say,

"I knew you once, but you fell away, and now you are lost." His words are clear and concise: "I never knew you."

So how will you choose—poorly or wisely?

"Nevertheless the solid foundation of God stands, having this seal: 'The Lord knows those who are His,' and, 'Let everyone who names the name of Christ depart from iniquity'" (2 Timothy 2:19). Here we see the evidence of true conversion: We give up our sins. There are three dangers that confront all who are hearing this message: a false pathway, a false prophet, and a false profession.

If you are on the broad way that leads to destruction, stop now and come to the Savior. If you have been deceived, remember that Jesus is the Truth. If your profession of faith did not lead to a change of life, come to the Lord now. Don't let the baggage of a temporary world deter you from the path to an eternal Kingdom. Leave it at the cross-shaped entrance to the narrow way that leads to life. As one evangelist said to me, speaking of a lost friend, "He may miss Heaven by 18 inches—the distance from his head to his heart."

THE SERMON

KEY QUESTIONS TO PONDER
Chapter 22: *You Have Chosen* _____

1. Read Matthew 7:13-23. What is the warning Jesus is giving in this passage of Scripture? Is He really warning us that wrong choices lead to destruction? Discuss.

2. There are many people who teach that "all roads lead to Heaven." Does this passage of Scripture teach that? Will some people expect to go to Heaven actually end up in Hell? Discuss how that is possible in light of this Scripture.

3. What do the "narrow" and "wide" gates represent?

Chapter 23
I WILL SURVIVE
The Life that Seeks Lasting Results

"Therefore whoever hears these sayings of Mine, and does them, I will liken him to a wise man who built his house on the rock: and the rain descended, the floods came, and the winds blew and beat on that house; and it did not fall, for it was founded on the rock.

But everyone who hears these sayings of Mine, and does not do them, will be like a foolish man who built his house on the sand: and the rain descended, the floods came, and the winds blew and beat on that house; and it fell. And great was its fall."

And so it was, when Jesus had ended these sayings, that the people were astonished at His teaching, for He taught them as one having authority, and not as the scribes.

—Matthew 7:24-29

Having begun the Sermon on the Mount with a blessing, Jesus now ends it with a warning. This warning takes the form of a parable in which Jesus sets for us a contrast. We have already observed the difference between *saying* and *being*. We might say, "Lord, Lord" and still be lost. This section begins with the contrast between *hearing and*

THE SERMON

doing. To hear the truth and not heed it is foolish indeed. To know the right thing to do and not do it is a prescription for disaster. Everything Jesus said on the Sermon on the Mount was meant to be the undergirding of our lives as believers. In Matthew, we have "the Great Commission" (28:19-20), which teaches us to reach out. It also says, *"teaching you to observe all things whatsoever I have commanded you."*

In the process of observing and obeying His command to reach out and build up, we must not neglect our need to dig down deep. We must find the bedrock of God's Word and let that be the support for the house of faith we are building.

The storms of August and September of 2017 illustrate this concept vividly. As hurricanes wracked the Caribbean, Virgin Islands, and southern United States, wreaking death and havoc throughout thousands of square miles, we witnessed the devastation of places like Cuba, Saint Martin, Puerto Rico, and Houston, Texas. With dozens of lives lost, and billions in damage reported, we still saw stories of courage and optimism. In the path of such destruction, it is almost impossible to come away unscathed, yet there were people who looked to the future with hope. Sure, they had experienced loss. However, in many cases, the damage was not viewed as insurmountable. When the authorities had called for evacuations, these people listened and left their homes and belongings behind, understanding the need to keep themselves and their families safe. It wasn't enough just to hear the warnings, they had to act: get in their cars, and drive for safe havens. Upon returning after the storms, most returned to a mess, but for many, their houses and businesses were still standing. Though battered by the storms, they had been built on a solid foundation, and withstood the fury and devastation that claimed lesser structures.

Where do we look for a solid foundation? How do we dig down into an unshakable bedrock? In what do we anchor our lives and futures?

THE FOUNDATIONS OF LIFE

It is interesting to note the various verses on foundations in the Scripture. In the verse before us, two types of foundations are mentioned—rock and sand—based on responses to the words of Jesus. The principles for living in the world are given in the Sermon on the Mount. These principles are a key part of that foundation.

So, lest we be confused into believing that the foundation for life is good works, let's take a look at several passages:

"Therefore thus says the Lord God: 'Behold, I lay in Zion a stone for a foundation, a tried stone, a precious cornerstone, a sure foundation; whoever believes will not act hastily'" (Isaiah 28:16).

"This is the 'stone which was rejected by you builders, which has become the chief cornerstone'" (Acts 4:11).

"For no other foundation can anyone lay than that which is laid, which is Jesus Christ" (1 Corinthians 3:11).

"Nevertheless the solid foundation of God stands, having this seal: 'The Lord knows those who are His,' and, 'Let everyone who names the name of Christ depart from iniquity'" (2 Timothy 2:19).

"Having been built on the foundation of the apostles and prophets, Jesus Christ Himself being the chief cornerstone" (Ephesians 2:20).

"Therefore, leaving the discussion of the elementary principles of Christ, let us go on to perfection, not laying again the foundation of repentance from dead works and of faith toward God" (Hebrews 6:1).

THE SERMON

"Command those who are rich in this present age not to be haughty, nor to trust in uncertain riches but in the living God, who gives us richly all things to enjoy. Let them do good, that they be rich in good works, ready to give, willing to share, storing up for themselves a good foundation for the time to come, that they may lay hold on eternal life" (1 Timothy 6:17-19).

When the presence of the Lord Jesus is evident in our lives, all of the foundations are laid. Layer upon layer, strata upon strata, the rock of Biblical foundation undergirds us.

Still, there are those who build their lives on the shifting sands of this world. Life cannot stand on the unpredictable sands of material wealth, because too often and inevitably, wealth will surrender to misfortune, ill health, age, and death. Life cannot survive in a mirage of temporary pleasure, for the momentary fires of passion and pleasure will always give way to the brutal force of the winds and rains of adversity. Life is unsustainable if powered by the energy of fame, because popularity is as fickle, unpredictable, and volatile as a desert sandstorm, covering over notoriety, accomplishments, and accolades as though they never existed.

THE VOCATIONS OF LIFE

Jesus makes it clear that everyone who hears His voice is a builder. That means you and I are builders. We are all building a life, and are all responsible, as individuals, for the site we choose to build on. Some foolishly choose a sandy foundation, while others aspire to build on that which is solid and immovable.

Anyone who has ever worked in the construction business understands the need to build with quality materials. In building a life, everything we do goes into the construction of our building—our life. Every thought we think is a brick. Every dream we dream is a structural beam. Every goal we set is another level of construction. Every experience is yet another picture gracing the walls of our imagination and memory.

Some people choose to use shoddy materials with which to build their lives. If everything you do goes into the construction of your building, what are you constructing by living a life filled with immorality? Are the pictures in the gallery of your imagination filled with sex, violence, and profanity? Are your walls supported by selfishness, greed, and evil intent? Were the footings sloppily poured with a mixture of indifference to God and slothfulness for His work?

So what are you building? A dwelling or a dump? A palace or a prison? A castle or a sty? The Taj Mahal or a tenement? What are you doing with the materials God has provided? Are you building a quality structure on His firm foundation?

THE EXAMINATIONS OF LIFE

The structure of your life will be tested. You can take that to the bank. However, I believe that this testing is both present and future.

Present Examination. Our lives fall under the tests of life's adversity. The rain, the floods, and the winds come to us all in this life. When times are tough, we discover what our lives are truly built upon.

Sometimes the storm may come in the form of a great adversity such as a serious illness, death of a loved one, family difficulty, or financial reversal. The test may come when we are faced with temptation. Look at the life of Joseph. He faced such a moment and ended up in jail for doing the right thing.

THE SERMON

The test may come in the form of God's call and will in your life. Abraham was asked to leave his home. Later, he offered his son Isaac as a sacrifice in response to God's command. While Isaac's life was spared, Abraham didn't know that would happen as he and Isaac climbed Mount Moriah. He simply obeyed the voice of God that said, "Offer up your son."

The test may come from many different directions in many different forms, but it shall come upon all of us. Whether we have built properly or not, the storms don't cease to come. They are coming, and all of us must face them. The difference is that only Jesus can keep us from being blown away by the winds of adversity. Only a life anchored in the Rock of our salvation provides the foundation that will keep our souls safe.

Future Examination. There will be a judgment for all. The saved will be examined at the Judgment Seat of Christ (1 Corinthians 3; 2 Corinthians 5). The building you call "my life" will be tested on that day by fire. Only what has been done for His glory will stand on that day.

The lost will be examined, as well, at the Great White Throne Judgment (Revelation 20:11-15). The evidence of a wasted life will be laid out before the Supreme Justice of the courts of Heaven. Great indeed will be the fall of that house.

A pastor went to visit a man whose wife had died. He attempted to comfort the grieving widower, but his efforts were futile. The man looked at the pastor and said, "Have you ever lost a wife?" When the pastor replied, "No," the man replied, "Get out, then! You don't know how I feel."

Little did that pastor know that, within a few weeks, his storm was coming. It was then that his own wife was killed in a train wreck.

At the memorial service, the pastor saw the man he had tried to comfort just weeks before. "Sir, I could not comfort you; I did not know how you felt," the broken pastor sobbed. "I know now, and though I am hurting, and I thought I would collapse under this burden, I have found that 'underneath are the everlasting arms.'" [65]

When all else had been stripped away, the pastor found Jesus to be the foundation that would not let him fall.

Friend, you were meant for more! You were meant for more than to just live a life "going along to get along." You are more than the 9-to-5 grind. Your life is more than marking time, waiting for Jesus return or an inevitable appointment with death. Anyone can just survive, but it takes the person living the Uncommon Life to what really matters, and what the "end game" is. With Christ as the foundation, we can do much more than just survive. We can thrive!

THE SERMON

KEY QUESTIONS TO PONDER
Chapter 23: *I Will Survive*

1. Read Matthew 7:24-29 and Isaiah 28:16. Discuss why Jesus compares those who obey His teachings to people who build houses on solid rock.

- What happens to those who build their lives on sand?

- What do the storms represent?

2. What does 1 Corinthians 3:10-15 teach about the judgment of believers?

3. Why are Christians tested?

Chapter 24
EPILOGUE
The Life that Is Uncommon

"All authority has been given to Me in heaven and on earth. Go therefore and make disciples of all the nations, baptizing them in the name of the Father and of the Son and of the Holy Spirit, teaching them to observe all things that I have commanded you; and lo, I am with you always, even to the end of the age."

—Matthew 28:18-20

So here we are, at the end of our journey together. But where this book ends, is where your journey, adventure, and Uncommon Life can begin! Now, lest you think the Uncommon Life will be a walk in the park, you might want to think again. While the Uncommon Life means peace with God, contentment, joy, and Spirit-filled living, you can believe it is going to get messy. In a world with a mindset conditioned to "look out for number one," and where self-aggrandizing reality TV shows and selfies flourish, those who choose the path of the Uncommon Life can know they will be at odds with a world that hated the One we have chosen to follow.

Taking up the mantle of the Uncommon Life is not merely a commitment to take up the sermon from Matthew 5-7; it is also a

THE SERMON

commitment to take up the cross of Matthew 27, which Jesus referred to when He said, *"If anyone desires to come after Me, let him deny himself, and take up his cross, and follow Me"* (16:24).

There are those who might have you believe that living an Uncommon Life is marked by all of the trappings of success—money, fame, and material possessions. But as C. S. Lewis said: "Indeed the safest road to Hell is the gradual one—the gentle slope, soft underfoot, without sudden turnings, without milestones, without signpost." [66]

That is not to say that if you have those things, you are going to Hell. Not at all. There are many believers God has chosen to bless with material success, and that is great. However, as we have learned in this study, material success is not the measure of the Uncommon Life. Not everyone is blessed with material prosperity, but every believer reading this right now has the ability to know and do the will of the Father, and live out the Uncommon Life with all of its promise, from this day forward.

I can say that living out the Uncommon Life while writing this book has been an adventure, both for me and my co-author Dana. In the course of writing this book, Dana suffered a heart attack at age 45. Less than seven months later, his appendix ruptured, revealing the fact that he had cancer. Over the next three years (this book has been a labor of love over several years), he was diagnosed with two more and different types of cancer. I can tell you, as his friend and his pastor, it hasn't always been easy for him. But Dana told me that God gave him a promise in 2006, and he chose to believe God's promise over a doctor's prognosis. And while there is no explanation for his history of medical crises, and his doctors remain baffled, Dana is still here, now cancer-free, and still trusting the God of the promise.

EPILOGUE

That is what being uncommon is all about. That attitude is the heart of the Uncommon Life; staring down a hostile world and an enemy that wants you dead, and saying defiantly, "I know who I am. I know whose I am. Therefore, take your best shot, but I'm still here, and I'm still following Jesus—no turning back."

It is choosing to believe the promises of God when there is no visible evidence to support that trust.

It's choosing to declare, "You are faithful!" in the midst of a friendless and faithless world.

It's abiding in the Vine when all of the branches around you are falling to the ground, broken and burned up under the heat of societal pressure.

It's standing alone in the arena of culture when everyone else around you are taking a knee.

It's loving Jesus passionately for all to see.

It's making the conscious decision to be an active participant in a world that is merely "phoning it in."

So, get out there! Make the decision to follow Jesus, to make His will your priority. Make the decision to let nothing hold you back from the adventure in store for you in your journey of faith and obedience.

Make the decision to be uncommon!

Endnotes

1. Bradley, General Omar N. "An Armistice Day Address." *The Collected Writings of General Omar N. Bradley, Vol. 1.* 584-589

2. *Homeless Man: The Restless Heart of Rich Mullins*, dir. Ben Pearson, Myrrh Records © 1998

3. Ibid.

4. Augustus Toplady, "Rock of Ages," 1763, public domain

5. Father Damien, also known as Blessed Damien of Molokai (January 3, 1840 – April 15, 1889). NOTE: For a comprehensive study of Father Damien go to the following website: http://www.newworldencyclopedia.org/entry/Father_Damien

6. Reggie White story was my personal takeaway from meeting him on set when I worked for the All-American Network during the 1990's/early 2000's. Stat information https://en.wikipedia.org/wiki/Reggie_White

7. Steve Taylor, "To Forgive," from the album *On The Fritz*, Sparrow Records © 1985

8. www.brainyquote.com/quotes/quotes/w/williampen

9. https://www.nytimes.com/2006/10/03

10. www.800padutch.com/amishforgiveness.shtml

11. William R. Newell, "At Calvary," 1895, public domain

12. http://en.wikipedia.org/wiki/Pope_John_Paul_II assassination attempt

13. http://www.newsmax.com/EdwardPentin/pope-john-paul-assassin/2009

14. *The Kingdom of Heaven*, dir. Ridley Scott, perf. Orlando Bloom, Liam Neeson, Eva Green, David Thewlis, 20th Century Fox, 2005

THE SERMON

15. http://www.brainyquote.com/quotes/authors/a/alan_k_simpson.html

16. Dietrich Bonhoeffer, *The Cost of Discipleship* (New York, NY: Simon and Schuster, 2012 (first pub. 1937) 112

17. Witness Lee, *Watchman Nee—A Seer of the Divine Revelation in the Present Age* (Anaheim, CA: Living Streams Ministries, 2007)

18. Eberhard Bethge, *Dietrich Bonhoeffer: A Biography* (Minneapolis, MN: Fortress Press, 2000) 927

19. Dietrich Bonhoeffer *The Cost of Discipleship* (New York, NY: Simon and Schuster, 2012 (first pub. 1937) 112

20. Elisabeth Elliot, *Shadow of the Almighty: The Life and Testament of Jim Elliot* (Grand Rapids, MI: Zondervan, 1958) 108

21. *It's A Wonderful Life,* dir. Frank Capra, perf. James Stewart, Donna Reed, Lionel Barrymore, and Thomas Mitchell. RKO, 1946

22. Randy Stonehill, "The Gods of Men" from the album *Love Beyond Reason* © 1985 Myrrh Records

23. Oliver Wendell Holmes as quoted by William Sloane Coffin, *The Collected Sermons of William Sloane Coffin: The Riverside Years, Vol. 2* (Google Books@ https://books.google.com/books)

24. Raphael Holinshed Chronicles of England, Scotland, and Ireland: Vol. 3 (1577)

25. *It's A Wonderful Life*, dir. Frank Capra, perf. James Stewart, Donna Reed, Lionel Barrymore, and Thomas Mitchell. RKO, 1946

26. Zig Ziglar, *See You at the Top* (Gretna, LA: Pelican Publishing, 2010) 35-36

27. Peter W. Stoner, *Science Speaks* (Chicago, IL: Moody Press, 1963)

28. Rich Mullins and Justin Peters, "Be With You," from the album *Pictures In The Sky*, Reunion Records © 1987

Endnotes

29. *Profiles of the Pacific* from the miniseries *The Pacific*, dir. Jeremy Poeswa, Timothy Van Patten, David Nutter, Carl Franklin, Tony To, Graham Yost. HBO, 2010

30. https//enough.org/stats_porn_industry

31. Bob Kelly, *Worth Repeating: More Than 5,000 Classic and Contemporary Quotes* (Grand Rapids, MI: Kregel Academic & Professional, 2003) 169

32. Frederick Dale Bruner, *The Christbook: Matthew A Commentary* (Grand Rapids, MI: William B. Eerdmans Publishing Co. 2007)

33. Naked Eyes (band), "Promises, Promises" from the album *Burning Bridges*, EMI © 1983

34. Ken Hartley story. Used by permission

35. *The Untouchables* dir. Brian De Palma, perf. Kevin Costner, Sean Connery, Andy Garcia. Paramount Pictures, 1987

36. http://en.wikipedia.org/wiki/Michael_Donald

37. http://www.encyclopedia.com/doc/1G2-3498200294.html

38. David Wilkerson, *The Cross and the Switchblade* (New York, NY: Penguin Books, 1977) 79-80

39. From Dana Harding's personal interview with his uncle

40. William Cowper, *What Various Hindrances We Meet,* 1779, public domain

41. http://www.worldinvisible.com/library/murray/praylife/prayer07

42. C. Austin Miles, "In The Garden," 1912, public domain

43. Michael McDonald, "East of Eden," from the album *Blink of an Eye*, Reprise ©1993

44. https://www.brainyquote.com/quotes/mahalia_jackson

THE SERMON

45. *Amos and Andy*, created by Charles Correll and Freeman Gosden, (WMAQ, Chicago (currently owned by CBS) 1920-1960

46. Corrie ten Boom, *I Stand at the Door and Knock: Meditations by the Author of The Hiding Place* (Grand Rapids, MI: Zondervan, 2008) 63

47. Joseph Menlicott Scriven, "What A Friend We Have in Jesus," 1855, public domain.

48. John Wesley quotes @ https://www.whatchristianswanttoknow.com/john-wesley-quotes-23-great-sayings/

49. *Mr. Holland's Opus,* dir. Stephen Herek, perf. Richard Dreyfuss, Glenne Headly, Jay Thomas, Olympia Dukakis. Hollywood Pictures, 1995

50. Charles T. Studd (d.1931), "Only One Life, 'Twill Soon Be Past," public domain

51. Rick Joyner, *Word for the Week* (Morningstar Ministries, 2005) https://www.morningstarministries.org/resources/word-week/2005/creating-clean-heart-part

52. Brennan Manning, *All Is Grace: A Ragamuffin Memoir* (Colorado Springs, CO: David C. Cook, 2011)

53. http://sports.yahoo.com/news/nfl—q-a-with-eli-manning—qb-talks-best-super-bowl-catch-and-roughhousing-with-peyton-.html

54. http://www.reuters.com/article/2013/09/16/us-nfl-giants-mannings

55. *The Patriot* dir. Roland Emmerich, perf. Mel Gibson, Heath Ledger, Joely Richardson, Jason Isaacs. Columbia Pictures, 2000

56. Charles M. Schultz, *Peanuts,* June 1980

57. Edwin Markham, *Outwitted*, 1913, public domain

58. William J. & Gloria Gaither, *I Lost It All to Find Everything* (William J. Gaither, 1976)

59. https://en.wikiquote.org/wiki/Daniel_Patrick_Moynihan

Endnotes

60. https://www.bustle.com/articles/152483-oj-simpsons-lawyer-robert-sharpiro-tells-barbara-walters-about-the-one-mistake-that-couldve-convicted-his

61. Frank Bettger, *How I Raised Myself From Failure to Success in Selling* (New York, NY: Simon & Schuster, 2009) 120

62. https://www.guideposts.org/better-living/positive-living/guideposts-classics-corrie-ten-boom-on-forgiveness

63. *Indiana Jones and the Last Crusade* dir. Steven Spielberg perf. Harrison Ford, Sean Connery, Alison Doody, John Rhys-Davies. Paramount Pictures, 1989

64. Adolph Hitler, *Mein Kampf* (Eher Verlag, 1925) Vol. 1, Chap. 6

65. Walter B. Knight, *Knight's Master Book of New Illustrations* (Grand Rapids, MI: W.B. Eerdman's Publishing Co., 1965)

66. C. S. Lewis, *The Screwtape Letters* (Geoffrey Bles, 1942)